For there is nothing hidden that will not be disclosed,
and nothing concealed that will not be known
or brought out into the open.

—Luke 8:17 (niv)

MYSTERIES OF COBBLE HILL FARM

Digging Up Secrets
Hide and Seek
Into Thin Air
Three Dog Knight
Show Stopper
A Little Bird Told Me
The Christmas Camel Caper
On the Right Track

MYSTERIES OF COBBLE HILL FARM

On the Right Track

SHAEN LAYLE

A Gift from Guideposts

Thank you for your purchase! We want to express our gratitude for your support with a special gift just for you.

Dive into ***Spirit Lifters***, a complimentary e-book that will fortify your faith, offering solace during challenging moments. Its 31 carefully selected scripture verses will soothe and uplift your soul.

Please use the QR code or go to **guideposts.org/spiritlifters** to download.

Mysteries of Cobble Hill Farm is a trademark of Guideposts.

Published by Guideposts
100 Reserve Road, Suite E200, Danbury, CT 06810
Guideposts.org

Cover and interior design by Müllerhaus
Cover illustration by Bob Kayganich at Illustration Online LLC.
Typeset by Aptara, Inc.

ISBN 978-1-961251-97-7 (hardcover)
ISBN 978-1-961251-98-4 (softcover)
ISBN 978-1-961251-99-1 (epub)

Printed and bound in the United States of America
10 9 8 7 6 5 4 3 2 1

MYSTERIES OF COBBLE HILL FARM

On the Right Track

GLOSSARY OF UK TERMS

aye • yes

biscuit • cookie

car park • parking lot

clapped the cat and the dog in the cupboard • secured the animals

cuppa • cup of

daffy • crazy, strange, or foolish in an endearing way

daft • silly or crazy

ta • thank you

two shakes of a gimmer's tail • quickly

wireless • radio

CHAPTER ONE

Harriet Bailey's day—a blustery Monday in January—took an unusual turn toward late afternoon.

"So, do you know what's wrong?" Teenage Oliver Hawthorne wrung his hands as he stood across from Harriet in an exam room. She normally didn't work at Cobble Hill Farm, the veterinary clinic she'd inherited from her grandfather, this late in the day, but she had heard the panic in the teen's voice when he'd asked for an emergency appointment. She could never refuse someone in distress over an animal.

Poor Oliver. One day into his first job pet-sitting, calamity had already found him.

Harriet placed a steadying hand on Signe Larsson's rabbit, Lilla. Then she back-combed Lilla's soft fur with her other hand so she could see the skin underneath. Nothing seemed amiss. She lifted Lilla's upper lip to see her teeth.

Harriet's thoughtful humming did nothing to soothe the worry on Oliver's face.

"What?" he asked. "What's wrong with her?"

"I'm not sure yet, to be honest."

Lilla was a juvenile English Angora rabbit, a breed known for their fluffy coats and bent ears. Lilla's vitals were normal, and she didn't show signs of infection, but her fur had scattered patches of slate-blue color. Most of it was in her undercoat, but that wasn't the only affected area. Harriet's original instinct was to check for a bacterial skin condition called *Pseudomonas aeruginosa*, or "blue fur disease." It was frequently caused by damp bedding or excess weight, but Lilla didn't seem to suffer from either.

She addressed Oliver. "You're sure Lilla didn't get into anything?" Perhaps the rabbit had been lying on something, like a blanket, which caused dye transfer.

"No, I don't think so."

"She's been eating normally? No new foods?"

Oliver shook his head. "All I gave her was the food Mrs. Larsson left for her. Fresh vegetables and timothy hay. Plenty of fresh water."

Harriet ran through possible scenarios but couldn't latch on to any definitive cause for Lilla's blue fur. "And she's been acting all right otherwise? No unusual behavior?"

"No, she's totally fine. No issues other than turning blue."

Harriet lifted Lilla from the examination table and cradled her in her arms. Then she directed Oliver to the clinic lobby where Lilla's carrier waited. Harriet secured the rabbit in the crate before addressing Oliver again. "She appears healthy. I don't see cause for concern, but I'd like to keep her for observation overnight. I'm also going to give her a dose of antibiotics in case we're dealing with a bacterial infection. You can come pick her up tomorrow, providing she isn't showing signs of any complications."

At this, Oliver's face finally relaxed. "Aye, right then."

Harriet supposed he was relieved to have Lilla's welfare shifted onto someone else's shoulders for an evening. She didn't blame him.

She was well-acquainted with Lilla's owner and knew for a fact that Signe would be none too pleased if something happened to her pet while she was off celebrating her wedding anniversary with her husband in Denmark. Signe's perfectionism made her the perfect owner for Lilla, as Angora rabbits required lots of specialized care and attention, but that also put extra stress on anyone who was in charge of Lilla in Signe's absence.

Harriet led Oliver across the room to the front desk, where her assistant, Polly Thatcher, waited. "You can finish up with Polly while I get Lilla settled. Then you can run back home and fetch some of her food. I don't want to alter her diet in case it would cause additional problems. Rabbits can be delicate, and Angoras even more so."

"I can manage that."

"Great. Thanks for coming in today, Oliver." Harriet patted the teen's shoulder as she passed him with the carrier. "And don't worry. Lilla is in good hands."

"Ta, Doc."

Harriet had picked up enough of the Yorkshire dialect by now to know Oliver was thanking her. "You're welcome. Be sure to tell Polly you'll be in tomorrow to fetch Lilla."

Harriet returned to the exam room and administered an antibiotic to Lilla. Then she transported her to the clinic's boarding and recovery area, where she transitioned her from her carrier to a larger crate.

Just as Harriet was wrapping up Lilla's file in her office, Polly peeked around the doorframe. "Call for you up front. It's your aunt."

"Oops. I haven't checked my cell phone lately."

Harriet's aunt Jinny lived close by in the property's adjacent dower cottage, where she also ran a medical clinic. She probably wanted to ask why Harriet was running late for tea. Tea was a tradition that Harriet enjoyed, but sometimes she had trouble setting work aside for it, especially on busy days like today.

Harriet hurried to the reception area and picked up the landline. "I'm so sorry I'm late, Aunt Jinny, but—"

"Hi, Harriet! It's me! I'm in England!" The voice on the other end of the line was friendly and familiar. But it wasn't Aunt Jinny.

Harriet gasped. "Ashley?"

Ashley Fiske had been one of Harriet's good friends in Connecticut, but they'd fallen out of touch since Harriet's move to White Church Bay in Yorkshire, England. Other than a few scattered emails and text messages, Harriet's normally talkative friend had gone radio silent when Harriet crossed the Atlantic.

"Bingo!" Ashley sounded triumphant. "Did I surprise you?"

"You certainly did. What are you doing in England?"

Ashley's cheerful tone sobered. "Oh, we needed to get away for a while. I had some flight miles saved up through work and figured we might as well use them. We're never promised tomorrow." Ashley worked in hospitality for a large hotel chain in Connecticut, a job that was a perfect match for her outgoing personality.

"We?" Harriet echoed. "Is Trevor with you?"

Trevor was Ashley's son. A pang shot through Harriet as she thought of the turmoil the boy must have been through in the last year. He had lost his father the previous spring. Jon's sudden passing due to a car accident still seemed surreal. Ashley hadn't even messaged Harriet about it. Harriet's parents had been the ones to break the news to her, and when Harriet tried to contact Ashley with her condolences, she was met with an answering machine. It was as if their years of friendship dissolved overnight. Or maybe they'd never been as close as Harriet had thought.

Ashley's reply brought Harriet back to the present. "Yes, Trev is with me."

"Oh, wow. That's a big trip for a ten-year-old," Harriet said. "How's Trevor doing? And you?"

If Harriet thought a nicely timed pleasantry was going to get her friend to open up, though, she was wrong. Ashley neatly skirted the question and kept the conversation shallow. "We're doing great. Trev's grown a foot since you saw him last. What time do you get done with work?"

Maybe it would take some time for Ashley and Harriet to find solid footing in their friendship again. Harriet could be patient.

"Just finished a walk-in appointment, and I'm wrapping up for the day right now." Harriet covered the mouthpiece of the phone as she spied Polly putting on her coat.

"I've clapped Charlie and Maxwell in the cupboard. Need anything else?" Polly asked.

"In the cupboard?" Harriet was perplexed.

"Sorry, I mean they're secured for the night."

Harriet smiled. Another regionalism to add to her ever-growing list. It sounded like the clinic dog and cat were safely shut up in Harriet's house, which was conveniently connected to the clinic. She told Polly thanks and waved her out the door. Then she returned her attention to Ashley. "Where are you staying?"

"The Windmill Inn in Whitby."

Harriet knew the place. It was a charmingly rustic B and B a short distance from White Church Bay. Ashley and Trevor would no doubt be comfortable there.

Harriet had another idea though. "Why don't you stay with me? If you're able to cancel your reservations, that is."

"Oh, I don't know. I don't want to intrude."

She wouldn't be intruding. Though Harriet had family in White Church Bay and she'd made friends since her move from the States, January created in her a particular brand of loneliness. With the hustle and bustle of Christmas packed away and the moors thrust into gray gloom, Harriet found herself longing for the welcome familiarity of Connecticut. There were plenty of gray days in Connecticut as well, but her parents were there. She could visit well-known restaurants and stores with a quick drive on the *right* side of the road. So many memories were woven into the tapestry of the place where she was raised.

Here, she still felt out of place on occasion. Moving to England had been wonderful in so many ways, but in quiet moments, she wondered if she'd made the right choice in uprooting her life.

Ashley was a welcome reminder of home. Besides, if she stayed with Harriet, they might be able to figure out where their friendship had gone wrong and mend the broken pieces together.

"Trust me," Harriet said, "you're not intruding at all, Ash. I'd love for you to stay with me. It would be like old times, rooming together at college."

"The reservation is fully refundable, and that does sound like fun."

Harriet didn't leave room for her to change her mind. "Good. It's settled then. I'll be at Aunt Jinny's in two shakes of a gimmer's tail."

"What?" Ashley sounded baffled.

At least someone was less acclimated than Harriet. She laughed. "It means I'll be right there."

"Oh. See you then."

Harriet hung up then pulled on her coat and braced herself against the wind as she stepped outside and locked the clinic door. It was quick work to make her way to the dower cottage.

She opened the door to her aunt's house to find a mess.

Aunt Jinny's normally cozy and tidy sitting room was cluttered with antique furniture. Her aunt was cleaning an armoire while Ashley flicked a feather duster at an old desk. Even Trevor was going through a drawer.

"Harriet, come on in. Mind your step." Aunt Jinny led Harriet through the maze of furniture to a clear space on the floor. "Sorry about the clutter. I pulled some old pieces out of a back room. New Year's cleaning and all that."

"And then Trevor and I showed up," Ashley added. "Of course, we wanted to help. When in White Church…" She shook her feather duster and sneezed.

"She's a real gem. Especially after traveling so far. She must be exhausted." Aunt Jinny squeezed an arm around Ashley's shoulders as if she'd known Harriet's friend for years.

That's Yorkshire hospitality for you, Harriet reflected with a grin.

Ashley shook her head. "I don't think the jet lag has kicked in yet. I feel like I've had a gallon of coffee."

"You're probably running on adrenaline. It'll hit you soon enough." Harriet swapped places with her aunt to hug her friend. It was so good to see a familiar face from back home. Although "home" wasn't quite the right word, because White Church Bay was starting to feel like "home" as well, with its own roster of familiar faces. Spunky Polly Thatcher. Generous Doreen Danby, who lived close by. Pastor Fitzwilliam "Will" Knight, whose serious, thoughtful gaze reminded Harriet of a hero from a Jane Austen novel.

"So, Ashley, why don't we get you set up at the house? It's a hop, skip, and a jump from here. I have some delicious gooseberry scones from my neighbor if you're hungry." Doreen was forever dropping off some baked good or other.

"Sounds fine with me." Ashley picked up her feather duster again and ran it over the front of the desk. "Just let me finish up this piece before I grab our suitcases."

"Here's the drawer, Mom." Trevor picked up the empty desk drawer he had cleaned and positioned it to slide it into the empty space in the desk.

But the day wasn't done yielding surprises yet.

A crunching sound could be heard as Trevor tried to push the drawer closed. "Hey, there's something in there." He pulled the drawer out again and peered into the recess.

Ashley set her feather duster down and bent to follow her son's gaze. "Oh, wow. You're right." She reached in and removed a thick stack of curled papers, which she handed to Harriet's aunt.

Harriet moved to look over Aunt Jinny's shoulder. "It's a manuscript. '*Tracking Lies: The Truth Behind the Great War's S&W Railway Crash* by Adelaide Evergreen.'"

Aunt Jinny pressed a hand to her mouth. "It can't be. There was a report on the crash?"

"What?" The significance was completely lost on Harriet, and from the blank expression on Ashley's and Trevor's faces, they felt the same way.

Aunt Jinny gently thumbed through the pages. "There was a railway crash here during World War I. I think your great-great-granduncle—his name was Rhys Bailey, and he was your great-great-grandfather Harold's younger brother—was involved in some way, but I'm not sure how. They said the accident happened because of damaged track. Loss of transportation set the war effort back a bit, and White Church Bay people were blamed. Blight of the Bay, as it were."

"And those papers tell the story of the crash?" Trevor asked, his eyes wide.

Aunt Jinny stared down at the yellowed manuscript in her hands. "Apparently, this tells the truth of it."

CHAPTER TWO

"Sorry, but who's Adelaide Evergreen?" Ashley broke the silence first.

"She's a famous British author," Harriet told her. "I think she's mostly known for her children's books." Harriet couldn't say she was especially familiar with youth literature, but she remembered the author's name from the cover of *The Train Ticket Mystery*, which was a favorite story of Aunt Jinny's twin grandchildren, Sebastian and Sophie. Enchanted by the tale of siblings who solve a mystery at a train station, they'd begged her to read it to them every time they visited Aunt Jinny during the autumn months.

"I didn't know Adelaide Evergreen wrote anything for adults. Much less an exposé piece, which is what this title sounds like." Aunt Jinny riffled the papers again, careful not to damage the fragile paper. "And how did it end up in that old desk?"

Harriet traced a finger along the top of the piece. "Your guess is as good as mine. Was this a family heirloom?"

Aunt Jinny nodded. "Passed down from who knows how many generations back. I'm sure it came from the main house originally and then found its way to the cottage as overflow. Judging from the type of wood and cabriole legs, I'd guess it was built around the turn of the twentieth century."

Ashley snorted. "The oldest thing my parents passed down to me was some plastic dishware my mom bought on her honeymoon."

Harriet smiled. White Church Bay had a rich history, and she was proud her family was a part of it. She remembered how she felt when she first arrived in the village the previous year. She'd visited many times before, but it was different settling in as a permanent resident. Moving here had given her the opportunity to notice a different quality in the air, a weight born of antiquity.

History was a thread connecting generations together. But did this manuscript from a piece of heirloom furniture reveal something about her family? Had one of her relatives known Adelaide Evergreen? What was the truth behind the train crash? Questions filled Harriet's mind faster than she could capture them.

Aunt Jinny's brow furrowed, and Harriet could tell that her aunt felt a similar curiosity.

"So what's next?" Ashley asked. "This manuscript sounds like a real find. Do you think it's worth anything?"

"Oh, I'm sure it is," Aunt Jinny replied, raising her eyebrows. "Though I don't know that we'll see the benefit of it. The first step we'll need to take will be to get the manuscript authenticated. A professional should be able to guide the process after that. Who knows? Maybe it'll wind up in a museum or a university."

"This is so romantic," Ashley said. "I already love Yorkshire. And White Church Bay. How could things get more exciting than this?"

Aunt Jinny smiled. "It is intriguing. I'll give you that."

By that point, it was well into the evening. Aunt Jinny invited Harriet, Ashley, and Trevor to stay for dinner. She had made one of her specialties, shepherd's pie. Harriet helped herself to a hearty serving, as it was the perfect meal to offset the chilly night outside. Ashley appeared to enjoy her food, and even Trevor ate a plateful, although he fastidiously removed the peas from his pie with his fork.

The adults spent more time chatting over coffee while Trevor skimmed the manuscript pages that Aunt Jinny had laid out on the table.

"He adores anything to do with trains," Ashley said as Trevor hovered over the pages. "He always has."

After the group wrapped up at the cottage, Harriet led Ashley and Trevor across the estate to her home and got them settled in the two largest guest bedrooms. Trevor fell asleep almost as soon as his head hit the pillow, but Ashley's jet lag still hadn't kicked in by nine o'clock. She sat cross-legged on her bed as Harriet brought in more blankets to fend off the Yorkshire chill.

"Thanks." Ashley took the stack of blankets Harriet offered her. "I can hardly believe I'm in England right now. It doesn't seem quite real."

"I'm happy you came." But as pleased as Harriet was to see her friend, Ashley's presence puzzled her. Why was her old friend here, and so suddenly? She'd shown up on Harriet's doorstep without so much as a warning phone call. "I was surprised to hear from you this afternoon though. I had no idea you were coming."

Ashley shrugged. "It was a spontaneous choice. Trev and I needed a change of pace."

"I'm sure. How are things back home?"

"Okay, I guess. Just a little stifling. Same old, same old, you know?"

It seemed like an odd way to describe life after such a loss as Ashley had sustained. Harriet would have thought the routine might be a comfort. Still, who was she to know what Ashley needed? Losing Grandad had been difficult, but nothing akin to what Ashley was going through.

So Harriet tried to be sensitive. She asked polite questions about Ashley's job, church, and social life. She inquired about Trevor's school and reminisced about people and places she and Ashley once had in common.

She was careful to leave some space in the conversation in case Ashley wanted to talk about Jon, but Ashley seemed determined to keep things light.

"Let's not talk about home anymore," Ashley said at last. "I want to talk about the here and now. I can't wait to see everything White Church Bay has to offer. Absolutely everything. This is a once-in-a-lifetime trip, and I plan to make it count."

Harriet gave up on drawing her friend out. If Ashley didn't want to talk, perhaps it wasn't Harriet's place to press. Everyone dealt with grief in their own way and their own time. Maybe Ashley would share more as she got settled in and they fell back into an old comfortable pattern with their friendship. Or perhaps what would help her most was a break from everything about her grief—both in her surroundings and in her conversation. After all, Harriet had no idea what kind of support system Ashley had at home. For all she knew, Ashley talked about Jon with someone else all the time.

Whatever the case, tonight's conversation would have to wait. Travel finally caught up to Ashley, as it had Trevor a few hours earlier. She fell asleep without revealing anything deeper than the fact that she'd forgotten her toothpaste at home and needed to borrow some from Harriet.

White Church Bay
Summer 1917

The first time Rhys Bailey saw Alice Wright, he thought he was looking at an angel.

It had already been a year of surreal occurrences. With the war in full force, German zeppelins filled the sky in spring. The waters crawled with enemy submarines and the land with tanks, even if most of the real fighting was focused south of Britain. Now boys not much older than seventeen-year-old Rhys swore their patriotic duty to their country and rushed to the front.

But not him. Though he longed for action—anything beyond the routine of schoolwork and farm chores that had filled his days since childhood—he was too young to fight. He could lie about his age to join up. Others had done it before him. A well-chewed old story circulated every so often about a twelve-year-old lad from a village not far from White Church Bay who did just that.

The boy served king and crown for two glorious weeks until his mam found out and forwarded his birth certificate to his superiors. He'd been unceremoniously shunted home, and the country had enacted a stricter rule, prohibiting men younger than nineteen from joining up.

Rhys's age had been a thorn in his side every day since the fighting began. But now, seeing the young woman's face surrounded by a cloud of cinnamon-colored curls as she plastered a war bonds poster onto the brick wall of the local fish and chips shop, he didn't mind. Maybe being relegated to White Church Bay was a good thing.

His school chum, Troy Chambers, elbowed him in the side. Troy was dark and swarthy from helping his dad on the family fishing skiff all season. Now, he followed Rhys's gaze. "She's right perfect, isn't she?"

Rhys suddenly thought better of drawing his friend's attention to the girl. "Exactly the reason why she's not perfect for you." He emphasized his sentence by timing a well-placed jab on Troy's shoulder. Then he hurried across the street, pushing his way past villagers waving tiny Union flags, determined to talk to the mystery woman before Troy could.

"Need help with that, miss?" Rhys positioned himself at the young woman's elbow in case Troy tried to cut in and edge him out.

She got part of the poster up before a corner peeled loose. She cast a quick glance over him before turning away. "No, thank you. I don't need any help."

Her cool response made him take a step back. He wasn't all ego like some chaps, but still. This wasn't the way he'd imagined the conversation going.

"I saw you eyeing me over there with your buddy." The girl leveled a glare over the crowd at Troy. Rhys's friend tipped his hat to her with a wide grin, oblivious to her mood.

Maybe ignorance was bliss. Her response almost made Rhys wish he'd stayed on the other side of the street. Almost.

She deftly smoothed the top corners of the poster back into place. "I know what you think. I'm some trophy to compete over, some conquest to win. Is that it?"

She had read the situation too well. Rhys tried to salvage the conversation. "Sorry. You're right. I didn't catch your name."

"That's because I didn't give it. Nor will I unless you treat me like a person instead of some prize in a contest."

"Fair enough." He thought for a moment and extended his hand. It felt odd, but it was the way he would greet a regular school friend or try to make a new one.

She appraised him for a moment before dropping her hand into his for a hearty shake. "Now that's more like it. My name's Alice Wright. And you are?"

"Rhys Bailey."

He basked in her glorious smile.

A light breeze slid under the poster. It peeled loose again and fluttered to the ground. They both lunged for it, but Alice snagged it first. This time, however, she allowed Rhys to help her secure it again.

A percussive cadence rose above the din of the crowd, followed by the sound of trumpets and flutes.

Alice glanced up the street. "That's the band. The parade will be starting soon. Should we go find a good spot along the route to watch?"

Rhys nodded, pleased that her cool initial reception to him had thawed. They made their way down a road that wound like a maze through White Church Bay. Shops and homes clustered together in the main part of town, and everywhere he looked was a riot of color—flowers in full bloom against cheerful buildings. Sometimes it was hard to believe that a war was raging.

Until he noticed how many men from the village were gone. Or the newsprint that blocked light from windows in case zeppelins appeared again to rain fire from the sky.

As he and Alice pushed through the crowd to find a good spot to view the parade, Rhys noticed Troy queued up at a table outside the millinery shop. The sign at the booth read RECRUITMENT.

A pang of jealousy hit Rhys. It had never seemed to matter that Troy was a full year and five months older, but now, the difference was more significant than he could express. It rankled to know that Troy could serve his country as an adult while Rhys was left behind.

Alice caught him watching. "Not old enough?"

Rhys gritted his teeth. "Not yet, but when I am…"

"Me too." Alice looked every bit as determined as Rhys felt.

He must have made an expression of surprise, because Alice laughed at him.

"I don't mean the on front, goose. I'm no Florence Nightingale. I mean, I want to do something to help the effort. I have a friend who quit school to go work at a filling factory up north." She sighed. "I just have to talk my mam into letting me do it."

Rhys understood her position. His parents supported the effort as much as anyone from White Church Bay, but there was no way they would let him abandon school.

"I aim to do my bit to help too," was all he said though. Alice gave him an admiring glance as the band began to play "God Save the King."

She put a hand on his shoulder for balance as she craned out into the street to see the start of the parade. The warmth of her touch sparked in him a longing to have a part in aiding the cause. Even if he had to go around the wishes of his family to do so.

And however he helped, he prayed it would be with Alice by his side.

CHAPTER THREE

Tuesday was Harriet's thirty-fourth birthday. The day sped by quickly, with plenty to keep her busy at work. Oliver came by to pick up Lilla, and Polly helped close the clinic as usual but lingered afterward instead of leaving.

"Mind if I swing by the house for a moment to say hello to your company?" Polly asked.

"Not at all. You're always welcome."

Ashley and Trevor were certainly getting a first-class welcome to White Church Bay. Aunt Jinny had rolled out the red carpet last night, and Doreen Danby stopped by the house with homemade bread earlier that morning.

When Harriet entered her house with Polly trailing behind, the lights were off.

Strange. Where were Ashley and Trevor?

Harriet headed for the light switch in the living room but didn't have time to do anything before the room was bathed in sudden brightness.

"Surprise!"

Her nearest and dearest friends and family stood in her living room. Aunt Jinny. Her son, Anthony, his wife, Olivia, and the twins. Doreen and her husband, Tom, and their five children. Ashley and

Trevor. And Will. They'd become good friends, though they'd recently admitted to feeling more than friendship for each other.

Harriet wound through the group, doling out greetings and hugs. Things were slightly awkward when she reached Will. She extended her hand to shake at the same time he opened his arms for a hug. They settled on an exuberant handshake.

"Thank you so much for coming," she said to him.

"Certainly. I wouldn't miss your birthday. I wanted to deliver your gift in person." Will's hazel eyes reminded her of sunbursts.

Harriet took the small, ribboned box he offered her. It was roughly the size and shape of a jewelry box, but he had just given her a necklace for Christmas. Surely he hadn't splurged on more such finery for her.

Besides, she wasn't totally clear on exactly what their relationship was. They'd held hands and confessed their feelings after a near-death experience three weeks before, but nothing had really happened since then. Will hadn't asked her on any dates, nor for any kind of romantic commitment. Did he regret what he'd said to her? Had he merely made that statement after confusing the intensity of his feelings after their scare? Was he trying to let her down easy by dropping the subject altogether and she wasn't taking the hint?

She opened the box to find two slips of paper. "You got me tickets to the London Symphony Orchestra?"

"Correction. I got *us* tickets to the London Symphony Orchestra."

"Just us?" The two of them had spent plenty of time together in town with mutual friends and chasing down clues to various mysteries. But this event would take place in London. The tickets weren't a spur-of-the moment decision. Buying them had taken planning and preparation and seemed more indicative of a date than a casual friend outing. Was Will testing the waters? Or was this nothing more than a friendly gesture?

Will smiled at her question. "Yes, just us. I remember you said you loved listening to the orchestra on the wireless during summer visits with your grandfather, and I thought you should get to see it live. Is that okay?"

"It's amazing," she told him, and she meant it. She was blown away that he'd not only remembered such a detail but acted on it.

"I hope you like it. I thought it would be an interesting way to experience more British culture together."

Did that mean he was invested in her staying in England? She tried not to let her emotions show on her face. "It's a wonderful gift. Thank you."

This time she was the one to initiate a hug. He seemed pleased, but she didn't dare ask if he was glad to have made her happy as a friend—or as something else.

Harriet spent the rest of the evening visiting with her guests and enjoying Aunt Jinny's delicious butterscotch cake, all the while trying to put the confusing situation out of her mind.

And never quite succeeding.

Wednesday afternoon, as Harriet was doing paperwork at the clinic, she received a text message from Ashley. FORGET TRAVEL JET LAG. NOW I THINK I HAVE BIRTHDAY JET LAG! IF A THIRD CUP OF COFFEE

FIXES ME UP, WANNA BUM AROUND THE BAY AND SIGHTSEE WITH TREV AND ME AFTER WORK?

Before Harriet could reply, another text pinged. This one was from Aunt Jinny. ANY WAY YOU COULD POP OVER TO THE MUSEUM AND PICK UP THE MANUSCRIPT? OLIVIA NEEDS ME TO GET THE TWINS FROM PRIMARY. THE MUSEUM CLOSES AT 3:30, SO I CAN'T DO BOTH. Olivia, was a kindergarten teacher, so something had likely come up at work to prevent her from picking up the twins herself.

The solution to this dilemma seemed simple enough. She could pick up the manuscript for Aunt Jinny and sightsee afterward with Ashley and Trevor. A flurry of texts cleared up the matter with both her aunt and Ashley.

Thankfully, Harriet didn't have any late-afternoon appointments at the clinic. Around three, she left the front desk in Polly's capable hands and hopped in her Land Rover, which she'd affectionately nicknamed the Beast. After a short drive along winding roads with Ashley riding up front and Trevor in the back seat, Harriet parked in one of the lots on a steep hill that led to the village.

When Harriet killed the engine, Ashley slowly loosened her grip on the handle over the window.

"You okay?" Harriet asked her.

Ashley's eyes were wide as she unbuckled her seat belt. "Pretty sure I white-knuckled it all the way here. How do you ever get used to driving on the wrong side of the road?"

Harriet chuckled. "I guess it depends on your perspective. If anybody from White Church Bay visited you in Connecticut, they'd think driving on the right was wrong."

Ashley laughed. "That sounds like the beginning of a joke." She and Harriet exited the car, but Trevor's nose was buried in a book. Ashley had to open the passenger door and prod him to get his attention. He reluctantly set aside his book.

Harriet squinted through the window to read the title on the book's cover. "Wow, you are quite the reader. '*Railroads Unveiled: A Journey Through the History, Technology, and Impact of Trains*' is pretty thick."

Trevor readjusted his glasses, reminding her of a little professor. "I've read this book three times already. It's fascinating." He unbuckled his seat belt and slid out of the car.

"I told you Trev was super into trains. Aren't you, bud?" Ashley wrapped an arm around her son and squeezed his shoulder.

"I love them," Trevor replied. "My favorite is a Central Pacific Railroad steam locomotive called the *Jupiter.* It was one of the trains involved in joining the Central Pacific and Union Pacific Railroads to make the first transcontinental railroad in 1869. People held a huge ceremony to celebrate the tracks coming together, and the final spike driven into the track was called 'the golden spike.'"

He rattled off the history easily, as if he'd talked about it a million times before. Harriet had to admit she was impressed by Trevor's knowledge.

A sudden gust of wind brought the scent of salt water.

Ashley wrapped her scarf tighter around her neck. "Wow, we're so close to the ocean here. Where's the museum?"

Harriet smiled. "We have a bit of a walk to get there. A car can only take you so far in this town."

"Fine by me. This place is really cute."

Harriet wondered if her friend would still be so thrilled after she had huffed and puffed her way back up the hill from the village to the car park.

After a bracing jaunt—which Ashley declared "refreshing after the gridlock at home"—they arrived in front of the Fisherman's Lane Museum.

The museum was a sculpted white building with a red-tiled roof that looked more like a charming residence than a place of business. In the summer months, the door was usually flanked by large pots brimming with flowers, but in the heart of winter, the stoop was clean and spare. Harriet reflected that January had its own kind of stark beauty as they pushed through the front door.

Inside the building, the welcome warmth of a woodstove took the chill off the air. Many of the downtown shops had been retrofitted with modern conveniences, but some retained their old-world feel, which added to the charm of village life. Most of the time, at least.

Harriet unwound her scarf from her neck. "Winters here are about as cold as Connecticut."

"I don't mind." Ashley's eyes sparkled as she studied a bronze plaque fastened on the wall. "It says this museum used to be a cottage. Then a vicar bought it on a one-thousand-year lease and converted it into a coroner's room and mortuary. Around 1900, it was used as a reading room, but—get this—was 'still used for its original purposes when necessary.'"

Trevor glanced over at his mom with wide eyes. "So this was a library *and* it held dead bodies?"

"Sounds like it."

"Wow, that's weird…but interesting."

Ashley looked thoughtful as she removed a small leather notebook from her coat pocket and scribbled some notes. When she saw Harriet watching her, she quickly snapped the book closed and tucked it into her pocket again.

"Travel journal," she explained. "Who knows when I'll make my way to England again? I need to keep a record of my trip."

While Ashley and Trevor wandered off to browse and further explore the small museum, Harriet approached the front desk. No one stood behind it, but a brass bell sat beside a guest register. She rang it twice before a woman rushed out from a room behind the counter.

The woman's name tag read PETRA MÜELLER. She seemed to be the same age as Harriet's parents or slightly older. Her dark hair was held back with a patterned headscarf. "Welcome to the Fisherman's Lane Museum," she said to Harriet. "How can I help you?"

"Hello," Harriet replied. "I'm here to pick up the Adelaide Evergreen manuscript that Jinny Garrett brought in."

"What?" Petra appeared genuinely startled. She consulted a note on her desk blotter. "Dr. Garrett said she was unable to stop by. I assumed she would pick it up tomorrow."

"Last-minute change of plans. She asked if I could pick it up for her. I'm her niece, Harriet. I took over Harold Bailey's veterinary practice last year." In White Church Bay, family lineage was important. It was amusing to find herself referred to as "Old Doc Bailey's granddaughter" as often as by her own name.

"Ah, that's right." Petra's features softened. "My condolences on your grandfather's passing."

"Thank you." A familiar emotion tightened Harriet's throat.

Ashley approached the counter and removed her mittens. Her wedding band still glinted on the fourth finger of her left hand. Harriet realized that even if Ashley wasn't ready to talk about it with her, the loss of her husband still affected her deeply.

"If you'll give me a moment," Petra said, "I'll fetch the manuscript for you."

"Take your time. I'm not in a rush."

Petra crossed the room and disappeared through a small doorway. After a brief wait, she returned with a thick stack of papers, which she set in front of Harriet on the counter. They were fresh and white, nothing like the yellowed and worn papers from the old desk.

Petra must have noticed Harriet's hesitation. "We made a copy of the document your aunt dropped off, and that is what we are releasing to you. It's common procedure, as it allows us to safely and correctly protect the original."

Well, that was unexpected. Aunt Jinny hadn't said anything about Harriet picking up a copy. "I'm sorry. I was under the impression that I was retrieving the original manuscript. Aren't those the rules under provenance?" Harriet knew that the word *provenance* loosely translated meant "history of ownership." Veterinary science was a more comfortable wheelhouse for her than legal matters, but she'd picked up a few phrases from her aunt's late husband, Dominick, who had specialized in property law.

Petra seemed much more composed now than she had on Harriet's arrival. She didn't miss a beat in her reply. "No, provenance doesn't apply in this particular situation." She rattled off a series of numbers that Harriet guessed was some kind of legal explanation.

"I don't understand."

Petra nodded toward the doorway she'd disappeared through a minute earlier. "We've called in a specialist, Robert Callum, who is a research lead from York St. John University. He has authenticated the manuscript and concluded that it is a genuine article, quite valuable. It would bring tens of thousand of pounds at auction."

Harriet stifled a gasp. The manuscript was more important than she had realized.

"The document is also of great historical significance to the Yorkshire area. This is why we're releasing a copy to you and not the original." Petra parceled out a tight smile. "Protection of an artifact overrides individual ownership."

"Are you certain?" Harriet pressed.

"Positive." It sounded as if there was little to no room for debate. "We're preparing to relocate the document to the university as soon as possible for its safekeeping, but we'll keep Dr. Garrett apprised as things progress."

"I see." Disappointment deflated Harriet's mood. Even though the copy would have the same information as the original document, it wasn't quite as intriguing as owning a century-old tell-all. But she supposed Petra knew what she was talking about. She likely dealt with similar situations all the time. It was important that the original document remain intact.

"Please be aware that the process could take quite some time," Petra continued. "We need to be sure that the manuscript is handled properly. It is absolutely irreplaceable."

Her last statement had the finality of a closed door, and Harriet wasn't quite sure what to say. She wasn't fond of ruffling feathers, and in this situation, she didn't have enough information to protest.

After all, she'd never found an antique manuscript on her property before. Perhaps the woman was right, and this was what the law dictated. The university would be better able to protect the manuscript than Aunt Jinny or she could.

Still, something in Petra's response struck Harriet the wrong way. The woman's demeanor had shifted almost imperceptibly, but Harriet detected it. No space existed in the conversation for questioning, and Harriet couldn't help but wonder why.

But she didn't have time to dwell on the matter, because a young blond woman burst through the front door, bringing with her another gust of frigid wind from the outside.

Petra broke eye contact with Harriet to catch the blond woman's attention. "Eleanor?"

The woman stopped in her tracks. "Yes?"

"Robert is waiting for you in the back. I believe he has some paperwork for you to fill out."

"Of course."

Petra swiveled toward Harriet. "Is there anything else you need?"

"I guess not." Harriet was disappointed to leave the museum without the original manuscript, but it couldn't be helped. She tried to convince herself to trust the judgment of the museum staff, who had certainly been through this process countless times. At least she would have the satisfaction of telling Aunt Jinny that the manuscript was authentic. That was exciting news.

Harriet bade Petra goodbye and headed outside into the cold with Ashley and Trevor. She paused on the sidewalk to try to call her aunt, but the call went directly to voice mail. She would have to tell Aunt Jinny in person. The three of them returned to Harriet's car, and Harriet set the copy of the manuscript in the back seat next to Trevor.

"Can I read this now?" he asked.

Harriet shrugged. "I don't see why not. It's a copy."

"Great. Thanks."

Trevor picked up the sheaf of papers and began reading while Harriet maneuvered the Beast out of town and onto the winding roads that led home. They had just passed a picturesque field of placid cows when Trevor's voice came from behind them.

"Hey, what happened to chapter eighteen?"

CHAPTER FOUR

Harriet glanced at Trevor's face in the rearview mirror. "What do you mean?"

"Chapter eighteen is gone. The story jumps straight from seventeen to nineteen. I skimmed that chapter Monday night when we found it, but I wanted to read it to get all the details. It talked about who caused the crash and some stuff about this family who sold damaged cargo on the black market."

Ashley turned in her seat. "Are you sure?" she asked.

Trevor handed the pages forward. "See for yourself."

Ashley thumbed through them then agreed with Trevor's assessment. "He's right. A whole chapter is gone. Trev, are you sure there weren't pages missing in the original manuscript?"

"Yes, I'm sure. I told you. I read some of chapter eighteen. It was definitely in the original." Trevor's voice was tinged with disappointment. "Aw, man. I really wanted to know what happened."

Harriet eased around a curve in the road. She wasn't thrilled to learn the manuscript copy was missing a chapter, but it was probably a simple mistake. Some of the photocopied pages must have fallen from the printer or gotten shuffled onto another desk somewhere. Still, she didn't want to hand off a problem to Aunt Jinny.

"Is it okay with you two if we run back to the museum?" she asked. "It's supposed to close soon, but maybe we can make it if we hurry."

Ashley and Trevor waited in the car while Harriet hurried down to the museum. But when she tried the front door, it wouldn't budge.

She yanked on the handle again to make sure she wasn't dealing with a sticky doorjamb. Goodness knew she had plenty of those in her own home, old as it was. When that didn't work, she knocked, calling, "Hello?"

She received no response. A quick peek through a window to the left of the entry showed a dark interior. She heard voices and edged around the side of the building to see if anyone was near the back door, but a row of hedges blocked her view.

"If I could just see," she muttered through gritted teeth as she tried to balance on a flat landscaping stone. Perfect—there was a hole in the shrubbery. She steadied her balance and peered through, only to find a face staring back at her.

She yelped and toppled off the stone, tumbling onto the sidewalk.

A man with a dark, bushy beard popped his head over the top of the shrubbery. He must be standing on a ladder, and he held a pair of garden clippers. She guessed he was a gardener.

Harriet did her best to regain her composure as she got back to her feet. "I need to speak with someone from the museum. Have they all gone?" The voices she'd caught earlier were fainter now, and she could hear a revving noise, though it sounded far more like a motorcycle than a car. It made sense, since traffic was largely limited to bikes and pedestrians in town.

The man cut an imposing figure at his unnatural height, though his expression was friendly enough. Even without the ladder, she could tell he was tall. "My sister, Petra, runs the museum, but she just left. Is there something I can help you with? I'm Garrison."

Harriet filled him in on the missing pages from the manuscript. "I'm sure it's a mistake, but I would like to have them. The chapter has something to do with a family who profited from selling items from the crash on the black market. It sounded so interesting."

"A family who sold items on the black market, eh?" As had happened with Petra earlier, Garrison's demeanor changed, his smile falling into a scowl. "My sister is quite conscientious. It's not likely that she made such a mistake. Perhaps the section was always missing?"

"I'm not sure," Harriet said, though she trusted Trevor's assessment. "I'd like to check on it, at any rate."

"I'm sorry. There's nothing I can do. You'll have to come back on Monday. The museum's closed for the rest of the week."

It took a moment for Garrison's words to sink in. "Wait, the rest of the week? I thought the museum was open through Friday." That was what it had said on the website she'd checked prior to leaving the clinic.

"Not this week. It's now closed until Monday. Good day." Garrison dropped the words like stones. Then he abruptly turned his back on her and disappeared behind the hedge.

"Wait," Harriet called after him. "Isn't there a way to get in touch with someone in the meantime?"

Whether Garrison heard her or not, he didn't answer. Harriet stood on the sidewalk for a moment, chilled and confused, until another voice called out to her.

"Excuse me, but I couldn't help but overhear your conversation." The same blond woman who had hurried through the museum earlier now stood nearby on the sidewalk. Her arms were laden with papers. "Maybe I can help."

Harriet walked down the sidewalk to meet the young woman. "Do you know anything about the Adelaide Evergreen manuscript?"

"A little." The woman shuffled her paper stack to extend a mittened hand for Harriet to shake. "I'm Eleanor Caldwell. You can call me Ellie. I'm a doctoral candidate at York St. John University. I'm assisting Robert."

Perfect. Ellie might know something about the missing pages.

"My aunt found the manuscript," Harriet explained. "Petra released a copy to me, but there are pages missing from it. Do you know anything about that?"

Ellie shrugged. "I'm afraid I don't. I arrived in town a few hours ago to get my employment papers set up. But you're welcome to come with me to talk to Robert. He's staying at the Windsor Hotel, which is where I'm staying too. Or you can swing by the museum sometime tomorrow."

"Tomorrow? I thought it was closed until next week."

Ellie frowned. "Not that I'm aware of. Or perhaps they're only opening it to staff and people from the university."

Was Garrison mistaken? Or did he want Harriet to believe the museum was closed? "I'd like to speak to Robert, if he's available," she said.

"All right. Do you know where the hotel is located?" Ellie asked.

"I do." The Windsor was a well-known establishment, conveniently located across the road from the lot where Ashley and Trevor waited for Harriet.

"Great. If you'll meet me in the lobby, I'll see about arranging a meeting with Robert. I'm certain he'll be able to help you."

Ellie walked with Harriet to the car park, where Ellie gathered some items from her yellow Volkswagen. Harriet returned to her own car to explain the situation to Ashley and Trevor. The Windsor Hotel was a few minutes' walk from the sea wall and was a tourist attraction on its own. "Okay if this is the extent of our sightseeing today?"

"Sure." Ashley's eyes twinkled. "We have a real-life mystery on our hands. I'd be a fool to back out now."

Newcastle upon Tyne
Fall 1917

Never had Alice felt so alone as she did that first day entering the National Artillery Filling Factory in Newcastle upon Tyne. She wished for the comfort of Rhys's familiar face. Had summer only been a few months ago? The memory felt more like a misty dream than reality.

When she'd first expressed her desire to leave home and go to the country's aid by working at a munitions plant, Mam had protested. Alice expected her resistance. After all, they'd already said goodbye to Alice's dad and two older brothers, and other than mischievous seven-year-old Jimmy, Alice was all Mam had to keep her company at home.

Inspired by the war bond drive and the slew of patriotic speeches and events sprinkled throughout the summer, Alice pressed her case with fervor. The sight of the German zeppelins clouding the sky filled her with a need for action.

So she'd traded her childhood for the required uniform of the factory—heavy apron, work gloves, and scarf to cover her hair. She clutched them as she stared at the outside of the munitions plant.

The building was imposing, a sand-colored block with a tall, fenced entry that reminded her of a gaping mouth. The stern-faced women and a few men who queued up outside of the place were even more intimidating. Some of the women had an odd pallor. At first, Alice thought it was the dimness of the morning light playing tricks on her eyes. But when the daylight increased and the women's skin still appeared yellow, Alice didn't know how to explain it.

Florence, the tall woman from Scarborough Alice met on the train, nudged her. When Florence had introduced herself, Alice remembered her words to Rhys on the day they'd met. I'm no Florence Nightingale, *she'd told him. And now she'd befriended a Florence.*

Her new friend had worked at the plant for a few weeks—she'd been on the train after a visit home—and seemed like a font of knowledge to Alice. "Right strange, isn't it? Those are Canary Girls."

Florence spoke at a normal volume, but Alice worried some of the women might hear their conversation. She lowered her voice to reply. "What does that mean?"

"Canary Girls," Florence repeated. "That's what they call them. Because of the way their skin has that yellowish color."

"What causes that?"

"Chemicals in the explosives we stuff into the artillery shells." Florence shrugged. "Most people who've worked here for a while have it. Nobody knows why, but it doesn't seem to cause any harm."

"Oh." Alice tried to smile, but a sense of dread settled in the pit of her stomach. What had she gotten herself into? Should she have stayed at home after all, helping her mother? But it was too late now to have second thoughts. She'd committed herself, but to what, she wasn't entirely sure anymore. "Stiff upper lip, lass," she muttered to herself as the queue continued to march toward the doorway.

A stoic guard stopped each person as they approached the entrance. His face registered no emotion, which was almost more frightening than outright hostility. "Any metal items?" he barked when Alice reached him.

Alice was so taken aback she didn't know what to say.

"I said, any metal items?"

"N-no."

The guard narrowed a skeptical glance at her. "Then what's holding up your hair, miss? Magic?"

Alice's hands flew to her hair and the bun she had carefully pinned into place in the wee hours of the morning. "Do you mean my hairpins?" she ventured to ask. "Are those a problem?"

"We have a new girl!" A stout woman three places back from Alice let out a chortle, and a few giggles spread down the line.

Alice's face burned.

Florence, spoke low in her ear. "Metal can spark fires. Even something as simple as a hairpin. We aren't allowed to wear anything silk either, because of the static."

Alice shuddered as her friend's words sank in. They were working in a TNT factory. One wayward spark could take out the entire plant and all the workers with it. She couldn't believe she hadn't thought of that.

She obediently untangled the pins from her hair and handed them to the guard before hurrying inside the building. She made a mental note to fasten her hair with a tortoiseshell pin next time. She, Florence, and a few other women were directed to a small room, where they stashed their belongings and donned uniforms. As they walked onto the factory floor, the acrid odor of sweat and caustic chemicals filled the air.

"Don't worry. You'll get used to the smell." Florence was a foreign creature when suited up in her protective gear. Still, her voice was comforting and familiar in a place so far out of Alice's comfort zone as to feel like a different country entirely.

You'll get used to it.

Alice rolled the words around in her mind as she took her place on the filling line. Wasn't that the entirety of the last couple of years in a nutshell? You'll get used to the raids. The rations. The missing family. Whatever it takes. You'll get used to it.

She was getting awfully tired of getting used to terrible things.

A large, hollow cylindrical shell came down the line toward her. Mimicking Florence's experienced moves, Alice poured explosive powder into the shell. Then she firmly tamped the powder flat.

"Easy does it," Florence cautioned. "Not too hasty, or it might explode. A girl did that last week and nearly died."

A sick feeling rolled in Alice's stomach. But it was too late to back out now. She might not be on the battlefield, but she was a kind of soldier now too. Scared but still willing to sacrifice what was needed. On and on, she followed the same process for shell after shell.

By the end of the first week, she'd nearly forgotten about the Canary Girls. They were ordinary women like her, working their hardest to serve their country. She didn't wear wire pins in her hair anymore and laughed when the guards startled new workers with their rules about metal and silk. The factory became her world, and the sights and sounds of White Church Bay felt like a dream rather than a memory.

She would get used to it. The war had forced her hand, proving she could get used to anything.

CHAPTER FIVE

As usual, Ashley was game for an adventure, and if Trevor had a book to keep him occupied, he was on board as well.

Pleased they were all on the same page, Harriet followed Ellie to the Windsor. The hotel's facade was a classic example of Victorian elegance, and its multiple stories featured a breathtaking view of the coast. The building was solid and imposing, standing strong against the ravages of time and brine.

They exited Harriet's car and entered the lobby of the hotel. Harriet had never been inside the establishment and was impressed by the opulent entryway. The space boasted a herringbone floor, gilded furniture, and a crystal chandelier that gleamed in the late-afternoon light. A metal coat of arms hung above the doorway that led to the check-in desk and added to the ancient feel of the surroundings.

"Not a bad place to spend a fortnight." Ellie grinned as she led them to a seating area inside the lobby. "I'll see if I can track down Robert. Be right back."

A short while later, she returned with news that Robert would join them momentarily. "Are you okay to wait for a few minutes?"

"I'm just along for the ride," Ashley answered. "No schedule for me."

Trevor seemed content with his nose buried in his train book again.

Harriet nodded in response to Ellie's question. The afternoon's unexpected errand had cut short her work at the clinic, but paperwork could wait. Polly would take care of closing for the night.

"So, how did you get involved with the museum?" Ashley asked the young woman.

Ellie shrugged. "I've always had a passion for British children's literature. When I finished my bachelor's degree, I didn't want to stop. So I got a master's, and now, I'm not far out from receiving my doctorate. Let me tell you—it's not just burning the midnight oil when you're a doctoral student. You're burning the oil at all hours. Anyway, my thesis focuses on the body of work produced by Adelaide Evergreen and posits that she died prior to finishing her last manuscript, which was lost to time."

"What made you think she had a missing manuscript?" Harriet asked.

"Some letters she wrote to her husband, Peter Kaplan. Theirs was a notoriously independent relationship, and he often conducted business away from home. She wrote a letter to him at the beginning of 1919 to let him know of her plans to take a writing retreat in a small village along the coast. She suffered from consumptive issues and hoped the sea air would cure her ailments. Judging from her descriptions, the town she traveled to bore a lot of resemblance to White Church Bay. Then when she mentioned she was writing a nonfiction piece likely to draw criticism, I was able to put the pieces together." Ellie took a deep breath. "Years of research and writing, paper after paper trying to prove the lost Adelaide Evergreen manuscript is real—and here we are."

Ashley raised her eyebrows, clearly impressed. "This must be so exciting for you, the culmination of all your research."

"It is exciting," Ellie agreed. "The document has caused a stir at the museum. Petra thinks it could put White Church Bay on the map. Working with Robert on it is thrilling as well. His reputation at the university is top-notch, and he worked for several prestigious museums before he came to York. He has quite an extensive background in detecting forgeries, so if he says the manuscript is legitimate, you can trust his professional assessment."

Time flew by as the women talked. But when the minutes stretched into half an hour, then an hour, with no sign of Robert, Harriet grew impatient.

"I'm so sorry." Ellie fished her cell phone from her tote bag. "Let me call Robert again. I have no idea what could be holding him up. He's always saying 'Time is money!' He's obsessed with saving a pound."

Ellie stepped away to speak to Robert, but Harriet could tell that the conversation was strained, judging by the tension in Ellie's back. Moments later, Ellie faced them again.

A smile was plastered on the young woman's face. "Robert apologizes for the delay. He'll be here shortly. If you have time, he would be happy to talk to you about the manuscript over dinner. The hotel has several places to eat, and they're all quite good."

Harriet's stomach growled loudly, to her embarrassment. "Dinner does sound like a welcome prospect."

"Great." Ellie's gaze swung to Ashley and Trevor. "And your friends?"

Trevor glanced up from his book and shrugged. "I could eat."

"Oh, you." Ashley ruffled her son's hair before sharing a bemused glance with Ellie and Harriet. "He's a preteen boy. They can always eat."

Ellie smiled. "All right. Dinner it is." She relayed the news to Robert.

Within a few minutes, he appeared in a doorway and crossed the lobby to meet them. He provided no excuse for his late arrival. He greeted Ashley and Trevor and then extended a hand to Harriet. "It's nice to meet you. You are Jinny Garrett's relative, correct?"

Harriet shook his hand. "Yes, I'm her niece. I'm excited to discuss the Adelaide Evergreen manuscript with you, Mr. Callum."

"Please, call me Robert." He dropped her hand to check his watch. "Why don't we get seated and order first? It's five o'clock, and the Arboretum is open now."

At his insistence, the group followed him across the hotel to a restaurant on the eastern side of the building. Not to be outdone by the lavish decor of the lobby, the Arboretum featured glowing lanterns, walls of windows, and skylights inset in the ceiling. The effect was a stunning panoramic view of sea and sky.

Harriet stood in the doorway and watched as the last sliver of sun melted into the ocean's horizon. "What a gorgeous sight."

"It's the most beautiful view. Well worth traveling from York," Ellie agreed.

A hostess sat them at a table tucked into a corner near the windows, which offered an even clearer view of the water and emerging stars. A quick scan of the menu showed numerous mouth-watering options. Harriet debated ordering seafood but ultimately decided on a creamy risotto with a fresh herb and arugula salad.

Harriet launched in as soon as she set aside her menu. The entire afternoon had been an exercise in patience. Robert had kept them waiting long enough, and she was eager to find out what was going on with the missing chapter. "Robert, I have some questions about the Adelaide Evergreen manuscript."

Robert leaned forward, planting his elbows on the table. "Why don't we enjoy our dinner first? We have plenty of time to talk."

Was Harriet imagining it, or had his jaw muscle tensed at her question? What was going on? Why was everyone she met today on edge about her aunt's find? It must have something to do with the content of the manuscript, and she was becoming more and more certain that the heart of it was the missing chapter eighteen.

"I'd rather not wait to discuss such an important discovery." The atmosphere grew uncomfortable as Robert didn't reply, but Harriet pressed on. "Can we talk now?"

Robert sighed and glanced at his phone as if he had somewhere else to be. Then he gave a short, reluctant nod.

Harriet got straight to the point. "I might be imagining it, but some of the museum employees acted odd when I picked up the manuscript copy for my aunt today." She explained the sudden shift in Petra's and Garrison's demeanors, as well as the sudden switch in museum hours. "Is the museum really closed?"

Robert nodded. "A last-minute change. They're taking inventory."

It sounded reasonable, though the timing was odd. "And the missing chapter? Can you explain that?"

Robert's jaw tensed again. "Do you have your copy with you?"

Harriet fished in her bag for the pages then handed them to Robert.

After a quick shuffle, he handed them back with a tight smile. "Yes, you're right. There are pages missing. I'm sure there's a simple explanation. Perhaps a copying error?"

It was an explanation Harriet had thought of, but the tightness in Robert's smile told her, as with Petra and Garrison, that there was more to the story. Besides, Garrison had told her Petra was unlikely to make such a mistake.

Harriet wasn't going to let it go. "I don't want you to have to take time away from your responsibilities, so I'm happy to stop by and help search for the pages if—"

"No!" Robert's voice was forceful enough that Harriet flinched. Then he lowered his voice to a normal volume. "I mean, no. That won't be necessary. We'll contact you when we find the missing pages."

Ellie opened her mouth to say something, but a withering glare from Robert silenced her.

Since they'd arrived in the dining room so early, the room had yet to fill with patrons. Their food arrived before Harriet could push any further.

Robert immediately became absorbed in eating his meal, but his body language betrayed him. Harriet could see his white-knuckled grip on his knife and fork. He asked for the check before he'd finished half the food on his plate.

Harriet's risotto was delicious, but she couldn't enjoy it. Something was going on. Everyone she'd met today had acted odd about the manuscript. But why? What secrets did its story reveal?

They sat in awkward silence as Robert rushed through his food. When the waitress brought the check, Harriet pulled her wallet from her bag.

Robert stopped her. "Oh, no. My treat." He sent the bill away with his credit card. "After all, you went out of your way for nothing."

His words were cordial, but an uneasy flutter filled Harriet's stomach as he paid for the entire table's meal. She had an odd feeling that the dinner was more than a simple act of generosity. Ellie had mentioned that Robert was tight with money. Why volunteer to foot the bill then? No one expected him to. What if it was hush money, intended to keep all of them quiet about the manuscript's missing pages?

Harriet almost rolled her eyes at herself. "Hush money" indeed. She'd been reading too many suspense novels.

Robert, Ashley, and Trevor struck up a lively conversation as they strolled ahead of Harriet and Ellie. Ellie snagged Harriet's coat sleeve and motioned for her to drop back from the group. "Harriet, I have to talk to you." Ellie's expression was pinched. "Something's going on. Earlier, on the phone, Robert threatened me."

Harriet's heart pounded faster. "Threatened you? What do you mean?"

Ellie glanced ahead at Robert's retreating form. "He told me to stop talking to you and not to ask any more questions about the manuscript. Do you know what he said?"

"No, what?"

Ellie's eyes were wide. "He said, 'Don't dig too much, or you might not like what you find in the dirt.'"

CHAPTER SIX

There wasn't much time to process Ellie's story, but Harriet encouraged her to go to the police.

Ellie refused. "I don't have any proof yet, aside from a verbal warning Robert can deny. Why don't you let me search at the museum and see if I can get some solid evidence before we involve the police. Okay?"

Harriet reluctantly agreed. She swapped contact information with Ellie, who promised to call her if she discovered anything.

Conflicted thoughts swirling in her mind, Harriet drove to Aunt Jinny's with Ashley and Trevor. The twins' parents hadn't picked them up from their grandmother's yet, and Harriet relished the opportunity to shower them with snuggles.

When they got inside, Sophie immediately sidled up to Trevor. "How old are you? I'm six."

"Ten." Trevor lowered his book and pushed his glasses up on his nose.

"Do you want to play checkers with us? I beat Sebastian, so you can play against me. I'm the rainy champion."

Harriet smiled at Sophie's words. "Do you mean, 'reigning champion'?"

"No. That doesn't even make sense." Sophie stuck her hands on her hips.

Sebastian scowled at his sister. "I don't care that you won. I don't want to play checkers, anyway. I want to practice my jumps." He climbed up on the ottoman and flung himself off.

Aunt Jinny snagged Sebastian in midair. "Just don't get hurt, love. Your mum doesn't want to be greeted by an injury."

"Okay," Sebastian agreed before climbing up and jumping off again. With her brother occupied, Sophie took Trevor's hand and guided him to the rug in front of the crackling fire to play checkers.

"Have you eaten?" Aunt Jinny asked Harriet and Ashley.

Harriet nodded. "Actually, we had dinner with Robert Callum, the research lead in charge of handling the manuscript."

"Maybe some pie then?" Aunt Jinny led them into the kitchen. "I'm eager to hear what you found out. The document's authentic?"

Harriet sat at the table. "It is."

Aunt Jinny shot her a questioning glance as she gathered plates and forks. "That's good news, right? You act like it's not."

"No, it's definitely good, but the situation has become complicated."

"What do you mean? I want to hear everything. But first, pie." Aunt Jinny gave each of them a thick slice of winter fruit pie. Harriet's aunt was a marvelous cook. The pie oozed warm fruit filling, and the crust was perfectly light and flaky.

Harriet closed her eyes as she took another bite. If Aunt Jinny ever decided to retire from the medical profession, she could have a bakery queue around the block. The momentary distraction of the dessert shoved the mystery from her mind.

"Out of this world." Ashley's words after her first bite put voice to Harriet's thoughts. "Can you share your recipe?"

Aunt Jinny wagged a finger. "Ah, family secret. Maybe Harriet will pry it out of me someday."

Harriet smiled. The secret ingredient in Aunt Jinny's pie was a mystery for another day. For now, they needed to discover what was going on with the manuscript. It took willpower to set aside the delicious dessert and stay on track with the conversation, but she put her fork down after a few more bites.

She pulled the copy of the manuscript from her bag and explained what had happened at the museum, as well as the uncomfortable dinner with Robert and Ellie's startling confession. "He's hiding something. And I suspect Garrison and Petra are too."

Worry pinched the space between Aunt Jinny's brows. "We should study the document we have and see if we can figure out what's rattling the cages." She divided the manuscript into thirds. She handed one each to Harriet and Ashley and kept the third for herself.

Harriet had briefly looked over the manuscript the night they'd found it, but now she dove into its contents with fresh purpose. She had the benefit of reading the middle section of the document and much of the story prior to the missing chapter eighteen. Adelaide had written her book in 1919, two years after the S&W Railway crash. Though the official ruling appeared to lay blame for the accident on track that had fallen into disrepair, Adelaide's manuscript told a different story.

The pages painted a broad backdrop of war and featured a complex cast of characters, from railway employees to passengers to citizens of White Church Bay. Chapter seventeen even alluded to a local family's possible connection to the crash, though no surname was given. The document implied that the family might have been in league with a German contact involved with the crash. Adelaide also hinted that the family had directly benefited from the accident, as they later profited from the black-market sale of damaged goods.

How frustrating that chapter eighteen was missing. It must describe the payoff promised by the previous chapter. Were the Müellers and Robert trying to suppress the name of the family who had supposedly been involved with the crash?

Harriet tapped the page in front of her. "I think this might be significant." She explained what she'd read about the mystery family. "Robert doesn't seem to have any German heritage, but the Müellers likely do. You don't suppose the Müeller family might somehow be connected, do you?"

Aunt Jinny wrinkled her nose. "Oh, I don't know. Quite a few families around here have German ancestry. It would be irresponsible to assume involvement based solely on that. Besides, Petra seemed so enthusiastic when I dropped off the manuscript yesterday."

"Exactly," Harriet replied. "But she hadn't read it yet. She behaved quite differently with me today. She was flustered when I arrived after you'd told her you couldn't pick it up. And you should've seen Garrison's face when I mentioned there was a family involved in the black-market scandal. He was quite friendly before that, but then suddenly he was like a stone wall. What if the Müellers are descendants of the people involved with the crash?"

Ashley froze with a bite of pie halfway to her mouth. "So you think Petra saw a personal connection, panicked, and yanked chapter eighteen from the document? Because it had something to do with her family over a hundred years ago? Why would anyone care now?"

Aunt Jinny frowned. "Heritage is important in White Church Bay, and the Müellers are a well-known family. I can imagine people would take offense to their ancestors being involved in the crash. They might not admit it outright, but once a person's reputation is tarnished, it can be difficult to come back from. You might be onto something here, Harriet."

"But how would that involve Robert Callum?" Ashley asked.

Harriet scowled. "I don't know yet."

The women didn't have time to continue discussing theories, as a commotion in the sitting room interrupted them. A loud squeal was followed by the scurry of Sebastian and Sophie into the kitchen. Trevor hurried after the twins with wide eyes.

"Nan, there's an ogre outside." Sophie ran to Aunt Jinny and buried her face in her grandmother's sweater.

"We saw him through the windows," Sebastian added.

Aunt Jinny smiled and smoothed Sophie's hair. "Is this a new game you're playing? Hide from the ogre?"

"No, Nan. It's not play. It's real," Sophie insisted.

Trevor's normally thoughtful expression had been replaced by fear. "They're telling the truth. There's someone outside."

"What?" Aunt Jinny leaped to her feet and rushed to the sitting room.

Harriet directed the children to stay in the kitchen with Ashley before she followed her aunt into the sitting room.

The curtains were still open, though it was fully dark outside. The first thing Aunt Jinny did was to pull the drapes closed and switch off the light. Then she flicked on the light by the front steps and lifted the curtains to peer outside.

Harriet followed suit—just in time to spy a dark figure in a flat cap and overcoat run toward the lane. It was foggy, and she could only see the faint red glow of a brake light. That was followed by the unmistakable rev of an engine. Then the person was gone.

"Did you catch the license plate?" Aunt Jinny asked Harriet.

"No, I couldn't see anything. I'm not even sure it was a car. It might have been a motorcycle. It looked like one set of brake lights." Harriet felt breathless. All she could think of was what had sounded like a motorcycle pulling away from the museum during her conversation with Garrison. Was that Petra leaving the museum? Or Robert?

And was it one of them leaving Aunt Jinny's now?

Aunt Jinny hurried to the phone and punched in some numbers. "Hello? I'd like to report a stranger trespassing on my property."

Ashley appeared in the doorway to the kitchen. "What's going on? Was someone out there?"

"Someone was in the garden," she confirmed, "but they got away. We didn't get any identifying information. I couldn't tell if it was a man or woman or anything about the vehicle."

"Do you think this is related to the manuscript?" Ashley asked. Worry creased her features.

"I don't know, but the timing seems too coincidental for it to be anything else. Don't you think?"

Aunt Jinny finished her call and entered the sitting room. "The police are on their way."

Ashley resumed her post in the kitchen with the children while Harriet helped Aunt Jinny check all the door and window locks.

Soon there was a heavy knock at the door. Harriet jumped at the sound, but a quick glance out the window showed no trespasser, only the flashing lights of a police car.

Aunt Jinny opened the door.

Detective Constable Van Worthington stood on the steps in his black vest and peaked cap. Usually, Harriet couldn't help but think how young he appeared, with his boyish, freckled face and affable grin.

His grin was nowhere in sight now though. He appeared quite serious as he spoke to Aunt Jinny and Harriet about what they'd seen. They filled him in on everything—the recent find of the Adelaide Evergreen manuscript and people's strange behavior over the discovery, Harriet's conversation with Robert Callum, and the threat Ellie had received from him. Harriet didn't want to go against Ellie's wishes to keep the situation from the police, but now that someone appeared to be stalking Aunt Jinny's house, she didn't have a choice.

"It's possible someone is targeting you over the manuscript," Van said with a grim expression. "Please take care and immediately report any other unusual activity to the station. We'll try to keep an eye on your place in the meantime."

His businesslike expression melted into a flush that exaggerated his freckles. He nodded toward the kitchen, where Ashley and the children were. "Sounds like you have quite a crowd in here tonight. Don't suppose Polly stopped by for a visit?"

Despite the seriousness of the situation, Harriet could feel her mouth twitching into a smile. The detective constable had harbored secret feelings for Polly for a long time, and she had only recently returned his affections. They'd been dating for a few months now, and Van seemed eager to spend all his free time with Harriet's friend.

"I'm sorry. She's not here," Harriet answered.

"Too bad." Van's disappointment was evident. Polly did keep a busy social life apart from her relationship with him, though Harriet knew how much she cared for the young man. "We were supposed to grab dinner tonight, but I had to pick up a shift at the last minute. I would've liked to have seen her."

Harriet felt a rush of sympathy. "I'm sure she feels the same. I think she mentioned something about getting together with her parents and brothers tonight."

"Family is important." Van appeared mollified. He tipped his hat to the women and stood to go. "Don't hesitate to call me if you need anything."

"Thank you, Van." Aunt Jinny told him goodbye and shut the door behind him. Soon, the pulse of lights faded away in the fog.

"I need to go to the house and check on the animals," Harriet told her aunt. "But I don't want to leave you here alone."

The children and Ashley came back out into the sitting room. Trevor and Sebastian played a riotous version of Rock, Paper, Scissors on the couch, which devolved into a friendly debate about whether the game was called "Rock, Paper, Scissors" or "Paper, Scissors, Stone."

Sophie stared out the window. When the little girl sat up straight as if she saw something outside, Harriet's heart hammered.

Had the trespasser returned?

CHAPTER SEVEN

Thankfully, the person outside was a more welcome visitor.

"Mum!" Sophie squealed. She ran for the front door.

Aunt Jinny stopped her from opening it until she could verify who stood on the steps. When she did open it, it was to her daughter-in-law. Harriet knew her aunt got along well with Olivia and considered her to be the daughter she'd never had.

"Was that the DC's car I met coming away from your house?" Olivia asked as she stepped inside.

"There was somebody outside in the garden," Sophie announced. "Nan called the police."

Olivia's eyes widened in alarm. "What's she talking about? Is everyone okay?"

Aunt Jinny explained everything that had happened that day, though Harriet noticed she downplayed the severity of the matter for her daughter-in-law.

"This entire situation makes me nervous." Olivia's words mirrored Harriet's thoughts. "I don't think you should be alone here tonight."

"I agree. Aunt Jinny, why don't you stay with me?" Harriet suggested.

Aunt Jinny waved her hands dismissively. "Oh, no. You have company tonight. You don't need me intruding on your visit."

"It's fine," Harriet assured her, and Ashley echoed the sentiment.

At last, Aunt Jinny gave in. She crossed the room to give Olivia a hug. "I'll talk to you tomorrow. Don't worry, love."

"I'll try. Promise you'll call me if anything else happens?"

"I promise."

Olivia and the twins headed out. Aunt Jinny retreated to the bedroom to pack an overnight bag while Harriet, Ashley, and Trevor bundled into their coats.

"Ready to go." Aunt Jinny reappeared in the living room. The four of them exited the front door, exchanging the warmth of the cottage for the cold, dark garden.

"This afternoon I thought England was charming." Ashley pulled her coat tighter around herself. "Now I'm a little creeped out. You don't think anyone would be waiting outside Harriet's house for us, do you?"

Aunt Jinny snorted. "Of course not."

"She's right," Harriet said. She tried to sound as resolute as her aunt, though experiences with past intruders gave her pause. But there was no need to worry Ashley over that. "Besides, I have enough animals at my place to sound the alarm."

The thought was a comfort. Between Charlie and Maxwell, as well as the other animals boarding at the clinic, any intruder would be announced well in advance.

They soon arrived at Harriet's home. "See? Here we are. No trouble."

Ashley looked relieved.

Her American guests headed to their rooms for the night, and Harriet got Aunt Jinny settled in.

She went to her own room to get ready for bed, straining her ears for any unusual sounds that might indicate an intruder. Finally, she fell into an uneasy sleep. The whole night, she dreamed of dark shapes appearing out of the fog.

"Van asked about you last night," Harriet teased on Thursday morning as she passed by Polly, who was typing at the front desk. The worry over last night's trespasser didn't seem so dire in the bright light of the winter day. Plus, she had a fresh cup of coffee. That made her feel like she could face anything.

Harriet expected Polly to be flattered, or blush, or *something*. Instead, she gave a flat, "That's nice."

"I thought you'd be pleased. I thought things were going well between you two."

"I am. And they are going well." Polly blew out a sigh. "Mostly."

"Uh-oh. What's not going well?"

Polly shook her head. "It's silly. I shouldn't bother you with it. I'm probably imagining things."

"Friends are for talking things out with. That way you don't have to feel as if you're facing them alone," Harriet said. "I won't pry, but I'm here if it would help you to talk."

Polly bit her lip, clearly thinking over the offer. Then she said slowly, "Van is great. Really great. He's practically the perfect boyfriend. He's attentive and thoughtful. It's honestly the best relationship I've ever been in."

Harriet waited, allowing Polly to continue in her own time.

"But he's acting different lately. He's always distracted, even when we're together. Haven't you noticed?"

"He's a detective constable," Harriet said. "I'm sure he feels overwhelmed with the demands of his job sometimes."

"Maybe." Polly picked at an invisible spot on her desk. "Or maybe he's losing interest in me. Maybe he's unhappy in the relationship."

Harriet stifled a laugh and hid her amusement behind her mug of steaming coffee. "Losing interest in you? I don't think so, Polly." Van was besotted with Polly, as unwavering in his devotion to her as the stars were to the heavens. Harriet didn't see that changing anytime soon, if ever.

Polly blew out another long breath. "If you say so."

"You don't believe me?"

"I want to. But I'd feel better if I knew for certain." Polly set her elbows on the desk and plunked her chin into her hands. Then hope crept into her eyes. "Wait. I don't suppose you would—"

Anticipating Polly's request, Harriet cut her off. "Oh, no. No. Absolutely not. I'm not getting involved."

"You didn't even hear what I was going to ask."

Harriet took another sip of coffee. More caffeine was required for this conversation. "Okay. I'm all ears."

Polly smiled. "Good. I was thinking that maybe you could talk to him for me? Find out what's going on—delicately. He might be more open to talking about things with you than me, especially if he's having second thoughts about our relationship and doesn't want to hurt my feelings."

Harriet heaved a sigh. "I'm telling you he isn't having second thoughts. He's smitten with you. I don't think me talking to him is a good idea. I don't want to get in the middle. Why can't you ask him yourself?"

"It's too awkward. Can't you help me out? Please, Harriet?" Polly pleaded. "I'll do anything. I'll even clean out the boarding crates."

"You do that anyway," Harriet reminded her.

"Okay, then I won't complain about it for at least a week."

All relationships had bumps in the road. While Harriet supposed Van could be having second thoughts, it was unlikely. Polly needed Harriet's support, but there was a fine line between supporting and overstepping.

Harriet sighed. "I tell you what. If I'm with him and *he* brings it up, I'll see what I can find out."

"I'm sure he'll talk to you. He respects you." Polly patted Harriet's shoulder as if the matter was completely settled.

Harriet excused herself to work. "I'm going to check on the recoveries. I'll be in the back if you need me."

She topped off her cup with fresh coffee and entered the room inside the clinic where she housed pets recovering from surgery or illness. Several of the smaller animals had knocked over their food or water bowls, and the sole cat under observation had scattered kitty litter far and wide.

Harriet certainly had her work cut out for her.

When it came time to put fresh lining in some of the crates, she grabbed yesterday's copy of the *Whitby Gazette*. As she unfolded a page of the newspaper, a headline caught her attention.

ANTIQUE MANUSCRIPT FROM RENOWNED AUTHOR FOUND IN WHITE CHURCH BAY

CHAPTER EIGHT

Harriet quickly scanned the article, hoping that something in the text would give her insight into the situation and why everyone was acting so strangely about it. But the article gave nothing but the basic details of the discovery, noting that the manuscript had been found at Cobble Hill Farm and was being examined at the Fisherman's Lane Museum.

Harriet finished cleaning the cages, made sure latches were secure, and washed her hands. Then she took the article up front to show Polly.

Polly was as intrigued as Harriet. They took advantage of an appointment-free morning to go over the copy of the manuscript. The two were deep in discussion over the possible contents of the missing chapter when the front door opened.

A woman with a steel-gray bob haircut and a slight slouch entered the clinic. A German shepherd was leashed at her side.

Harriet approached the woman. "Hello, I'm Dr. Bailey. How can I help you?"

"Judith Martin." The woman rested a wrinkled hand on the dog's head. "This is my Alsatian, Magnus."

Many locals used the term Alsatian instead of German shepherd, a leftover relic of war sentiment that hadn't faded away.

"Do you have time for a walk-in appointment for us?" Judith asked.

"I think so. Polly?" Harriet asked.

"No problem," Polly replied. "It's good to see you again, Judith." This was Polly's way of letting Harriet know that Judith was a repeat client, so if Harriet hadn't seen her, that meant her grandfather had.

"What's going on with Magnus today?" Harriet asked.

Judith's gaze flicked toward the dog then up again to Harriet. "It's his stomach. He won't eat, and I'm concerned that he might have gotten into something."

"Poor fellow." Harriet held her hand out for Magnus to sniff before she patted his head. She glanced over at Polly. "Good to go on paperwork?"

"Everything's updated." Polly held up the manuscript. "Want me to put this back in your study when I'm done?"

"Yes, thanks."

Harriet turned her attention to Judith again. "Let's take Magnus to the back."

Judith followed Harriet to an empty exam room. "I noticed a *Whitby Gazette* on Polly's desk when I came in. I read about the Adelaide Evergreen manuscript in yesterday's paper. That book is quite a find, eh?"

"It certainly is." Harriet listened to Magnus's heart then his lungs. All seemed normal.

"Do you know anything about the manuscript?" Judith asked. "The paper said it was found on your property."

"It was found in my aunt's cottage." Harriet felt Magnus's stomach to check for any obstructions but found nothing.

"Yes, but I thought the paper said that someone took it to the museum."

Harriet fought distraction as Judith continued with her litany of questions. She really needed to focus on her patient right now, not the manuscript. But this was part of the job. People felt awkward standing silently while she poked and prodded their pet.

"The paper is right. The manuscript is at Fisherman's Lane."

"Then what was your receptionist reading out there? Sure looked like a book to me."

Had Judith been taking notes or something? Harriet started to feel slightly unsettled, the way she'd felt with the Müellers and Robert. Apparently, Adelaide's manuscript was bringing everyone out of the woodwork. She tried to steer the conversation back on track.

"So, I've finished examining Magnus. I don't see the source of his stomach issues yet. Our next step could be bloodwork. Or a scan if you think he ate a foreign object."

"Ah, no. No need for anything invasive." Judith wrung her hands. It wasn't an unusual response. People often got upset when they thought a beloved pet was ill. At least Judith had dropped her previous topic of discussion.

Harriet hurried to reassure Judith that the dog wasn't in distress but didn't get far into her speech before Polly stepped into the room.

"Sorry to interrupt, but Van is here."

"What's he doing here?" Judith's eyes widened.

Harriet's mind spun. Had Van found the person who was skulking in the shadows outside Aunt Jinny's cottage last night?

"I'm sure it's a simple courtesy call," Harriet told Judith. "Excuse me. I'll be right back, and I'll bring you some information on upset stomach in dogs."

"Okay."

Harriet joined Polly in the hallway, closing the exam room door behind her. "Why is Van here? Does he have news about the trespasser?"

"I think so. He said something about a lead."

"Great." Harriet started toward the lobby, but Polly lingered in the hallway. "What? What's wrong?"

"You go up front without me. I can print the information for Judith."

"No, that's fine. It will only take me a second to print it. Come up and talk to Van. I'm sure he would like to see you."

"I can't." Polly shook her head. "It's too awkward, Harriet."

Harriet frowned. "Suit yourself. Thanks for getting the information for Judith."

"Sure."

Harriet went up front to greet the detective constable. "Good morning, Van. What brings you by today?"

He adjusted his hat. "Just on patrol. No more unusual sightings, I hope?"

Harriet's shoulders relaxed a little. "No, thank goodness. Polly said you might have a lead regarding who was outside my aunt's cottage last night."

"Possibly. We nabbed a cat burglar who broke into a house a few miles away. The suspect is in custody now. We're still gathering information, but that person may have been casing your aunt's cottage. I'll let you know when we reach a more definitive conclusion."

"I'd appreciate that." Harriet felt a sense of relief. Perhaps the whole situation was as simple as that and she was imagining suspicious behavior related to the manuscript.

Van continued. "It's a good thing I was in the area, because I also have something I'd like to talk to Polly about. Any chance she's coming back out to the desk?"

"I'm not sure," Harriet answered. "She's printing some papers and running them to a patient for me."

"Oh." Van's face fell. "I suppose I'll catch her later. Would you let her know I'd like to chat with her?"

The sudden sound of dogs barking from the back of the clinic yanked Harriet from the conversation. She raced to the boarding area, Van on her heels.

A horrible sight met her eyes. Two of the dogs she had secured in separate crates were loose and fighting. Snapping teeth and flashing fur dominated the space.

Harriet was terrified they would wound each other. "Van, will you help me?" She directed the detective constable, and soon the growling dogs were safely separated.

Much to her relief, a quick check showed the only damage done was to everyone's nerves. Harriet soothed the dogs before securing them in their crates again. Then she led Van back into the empty reception area.

"I don't know how that could have happened," Harriet said. She was certain she had latched the crates. "Thanks so much for your help."

"Of course. I'm happy to be of assistance."

After a few more awkward moments of Van obviously waiting for Polly, he said a reluctant goodbye and left.

Polly peeked around the corner. "Is he gone?"

Harriet nodded. "He said he wanted to chat with you, though, when you have time."

"I wonder what that's about." Polly extended a piece of paper toward Harriet. "Here's the information for Judith."

The mention of the woman's name shook Harriet back to reality. All the commotion had distracted her from what she'd originally been doing—assessing Magnus. A low whine and a few short barks came from the direction of the exam room.

"I'm so sorry about your wait and the commotion," Harriet said as she entered the room where she had left her client. She stopped short as she realized she was talking to thin air.

Judith was nowhere to be seen. Magnus whined softly again, his leash wound around a table leg.

Harriet closed the door so the dog wouldn't escape and ventured out into the hallway. "Judith? Hello?"

She didn't see her, so she walked to the rear of the clinic. It was unlikely that Judith had wandered there, but sometimes people got turned around if they were searching for the restroom. "Judith?"

"Yes?" Judith's voice came from the direction of the storage room.

Harriet hurried toward the sound to find Judith standing uncertainly in the middle of the space. "What are you doing back here?"

"I was looking for the loo."

A simple explanation, as Harriet had expected. She showed Judith to the restroom. Then she finished up the appointment with

Magnus. She couldn't find anything wrong with the dog and released him with a prescription for a nausea medication. "Please call me if he doesn't start eating normally again. We can always pursue some of the other options I mentioned."

"All right. Thanks, Doc."

Harriet said goodbye to Judith and headed back to the storage area to shut off the lights and close the door. When she did so, however, she noticed that another door was open. The one leading into her home study.

Now she knew she wasn't imagining things. She definitely hadn't left the door open when she came into the clinic that morning. But if she hadn't opened it, who had?

Harriet stepped into her study and saw that papers were scattered on the floor by her desk. She crossed the room to pick them up. They were pages from the copy of the manuscript that Polly had returned to her desk, and the rest of the stack was messy, as if it had been hastily riffled through. Polly wouldn't have left the manuscript so untidy.

Harriet thought back to Judith's excuse that she was looking for the restroom and wound up in the storage area. But the woman had been to this clinic before. So why did she get lost on the way to the restroom? And then there was the fact that Magnus hadn't seemed ill at all.

When she got a break in appointments, Harriet called Ashley to ask if either she or Trevor had gone into her study and messed with the manuscript while Harriet was working.

"No, I didn't," was Ashley's response. "And Trevor has been reading one of his train books."

Harriet disconnected the call with a flicker of worry. Was it possible Judith had visited the clinic for reasons unrelated to her pet?

CHAPTER NINE

The rest of Thursday and Friday passed quickly. Between clinic appointments, Harriet tried to contact Judith but got her answering machine. She left Judith a vague message about needing her to call the clinic at her earliest convenience though, truth be told, she had no idea what to say to her if she did call back. Accusing a client of breaking and entering didn't seem like the best way to start a conversation.

But Judith didn't return Harriet's call.

Saturday morning Harriet awoke, unsure of what to do. She was still waiting for Ellie to contact her about the missing chapter. She'd reached a dead end. Maybe she needed a break from the mystery.

She resolved to take Ashley and Trevor on an official tour of White Church Bay as soon as she finished morning hours at the clinic, since they hadn't gotten to sightsee much yet. She got dressed and went downstairs to find Ashley already in the kitchen.

"I hope you don't mind me making myself at home." Ashley cut a couple of slices from a loaf of Doreen's bread. Her travel journal sat on the counter beside her. "Do you still like smash toast?"

Harriet hadn't thought about smash toast in years. When she and Ashley were roommates in college, it was one of their favorite late-night study snacks. Peanut butter mixed with smashed—not sliced—banana. The *smash* part of the recipe was important. Smashing the bananas brought out their sweetness, creating a better contrast with the salty peanut butter. Plus, this was the first time Ashley had willingly brought up the past. Even a nod to a college tradition felt like a step in the right direction with their friendship.

"Smash toast sounds great," Harriet said. She busied herself making coffee while Ashley took the toast from the toaster and spread each piece with a generous layer of peanut butter. Then she smashed some bananas in a bowl and added that to the toast as well, along with a generous drizzle of honey. It seemed like an odd toast topping choice, but it really wasn't that different from peanut butter and jelly.

With breakfast ready, the two friends sat in companionable silence while they ate and sipped their coffee. Soon, Ashley grabbed her journal and began scribbling in it.

"I hope you're writing about something more exciting than smash toast," Harriet teased.

She thought Ashley would laugh, but instead, she quickly shut the book and stood to her feet. "I didn't realize how late it was. Better go get ready."

Harriet tried to recapture the friendly ease they'd shared moments before. "I didn't mean to pry."

"No, it's fine." Ashley's words gave grace, but her smile was tight. She carried her dirty dishes to the sink, grabbed her journal, and left.

Before long, Trevor stumbled into the kitchen in his pajamas. He rubbed his eyes. "What are you making?"

"Smash toast. It's something your mom and I used to eat in college." While he got settled at the table, she prepared another helping and slid it in front of him.

As picky as Harriet knew kids could be, she was certain he would turn up his nose. But he gobbled down three helpings and a tall glass of milk without batting an eye.

"I didn't think you'd like smash toast," Harriet commented as he popped the last bite in his mouth.

Trevor chewed and swallowed. "Mom makes it at home a lot. She told me you guys used to have it all the time in school. She misses you."

"Really?" Harriet had a sudden vision of Ashley in her kitchen in Connecticut, reminiscing about college days and happy times long gone.

As difficult as Harriet's broken engagement had been, Ashley was going through something even worse. Finding a great love and then losing him. At least Harriet was able to mourn her loss with a clean start in England. She was missing the familiarity of Connecticut this winter, but she hadn't thought about how familiarity could bring pain as well as comfort. Every day, Ashley drove on roads that held memories of Jon. Shopped in stores that reminded her of him. Forced a brave face for everyone she saw, even with her world in tatters.

Trevor nodded in response to Harriet's question. "Yeah. Mom talks all the time about the fun stuff you guys used to do together. She doesn't really have a best friend back home."

That was news to Harriet. But then again, it made sense. Ashley was a social butterfly, flitting effortlessly between social interactions. While her bubbly personality gained her many new friends, maybe she found it difficult to go deeper than surface level with them.

But if Harriet was her closest friend, why wouldn't she open up to her? What secrets was she baring to her journal that she couldn't reveal to Harriet?

Fortified by smash toast and coffee, Harriet worked until noon at the clinic. Then she took Ashley and Trevor out sightseeing. It was a beautiful, clear afternoon, and though it was cold, the wind was relatively mild. Harriet spent several hours showing Ashley and Trevor the best White Church Bay had to offer, including the expansive view from the sea wall and the quaint shops crowding cobblestone streets in town.

"Oh, let's go in this one," Ashley said as they passed by a cozy storefront. "I still need to get some toothpaste."

The three of them ducked into the shop. Harriet browsed absentmindedly as Ashley went off in search of toiletries. She was absorbed in studying a spinner rack of postcards when someone bumped into her. Harriet glanced up to see Ellie Caldwell's surprised face. The young woman looked frazzled and more than a little sleep deprived.

"Harriet." Ellie smoothed her hair back from her face. "I was planning to call you today. What are you doing here?"

Harriet leaned down to retrieve a postcard that had fluttered to the ground. "I'm showing Ashley and Trevor around town. It's a beautiful day for it. How about you? No work at the museum?"

Ellie shook her head. "No, not today. I'm running some errands and stocking up on essentials. Also working on my thesis, of course. But speaking of the museum…"

"What? Did you find out something?"

"Sort of." Ellie bit her bottom lip. "I tried to talk to Robert, but he wouldn't give me much information. He just told me the same thing as before—that I need to do my job and not ask questions."

"Is chapter eighteen still missing? Or did you find it?"

"It's not missing." Ellie bit her lip again and seemed hesitant to continue talking.

"That's great news," Harriet said.

But Ellie's expression told a different story. "Not so great, actually. I found the missing chapter on Robert's desk. It looked like he was making a copy of it."

"Like on a copy machine?"

"No, no." Ellie's voice lowered to a whisper. "Like a forgery, with aged pages and everything. Remember I told you that he used to work for a museum and specialized in forgery detection?"

"Yes."

"Well, it seems his skill extends further than I thought. He can make forgeries as well as identify them. I also saw an uncashed check under a stack of file folders. It was made out to Robert from Petra and was written for a significant amount of money."

Harriet was speechless. Why would Robert forge a copy of chapter eighteen? Were the Müellers bribing him to cover up information? Were the three of them literally trying to rewrite history?

Ellie continued. "And if that doesn't convince you, I also overheard a conversation between the Müellers. Petra told Garrison that she intended to squash every scrap of incriminating evidence against their family. She said she needed Garrison's help to track down any other localized information about the crash and destroy it."

That confirmed Harriet's earlier suspicions. The Müellers and Robert were keeping chapter eighteen from prying eyes for selfish reasons. Ellie's words brought up another point as well. Harriet hadn't considered that there might be other information referencing the crash.

"Listen, Ellie. Could you do me a favor?"

"It depends on what it is."

"It's imperative. Track down the *real* chapter eighteen and take it to the police. We must get them involved now. We need to know what everyone's trying to cover up."

"I don't know if I can do that."

"Why not?" Ellie had been completely on board before.

"It's one thing to scout the situation," Ellie explained. "It's another matter entirely to remove papers from the museum. I don't have authorization to do that. What if I'm wrong about things? What if it's a misunderstanding? That's something I could be held liable for. I could lose this internship and my position at the university. I can't risk it."

Harriet understood Ellie's concerns. They were valid, but there was more than one way to approach things. "Can you send me pictures of the chapter, so we'll have digital proof? Don't you want to know the truth?"

"Of course. My entire thesis is dedicated to discovering the truth about Adelaide Evergreen and her manuscript." Ellie sighed. "I'll see what I can do. But no promises."

"Fair enough." Harriet thanked Ellie then found Ashley and Trevor again. Trevor had apparently talked his mom into a box of gumballs, and he clutched them like a prize.

"Found what I was looking for." Ashley held up a tube of toothpaste. "It's not my usual brand, but it'll do. Was that Ellie you were talking to?"

Harriet nodded and filled Ashley in on the information Ellie had revealed. They finished sightseeing and returned home, windswept and weary.

The mystery was deepening, and Harriet couldn't say she was happy about it. At least now she had her next foothold. She needed to find out why the Müeller siblings were upset about Harriet's investigation. They were a long-standing family in White Church Bay. They and their ancestors had contributed much to the village. But was it possible the family's past wasn't as spotless as it first appeared?

The only way they would find out was if Ellie came through.

CHAPTER TEN

White Church Bay
Winter 1917

The afternoon was bitterly cold, and skiffs of pale snow colored the cliffs along the coastline. Rhys pulled his woolen overcoat tighter as he walked up the steps and entered the welcome warmth of the station.

"Need a ticket?" The ticket master stood behind a window on Rhys's right. Wooden posts flanked the approach to the counter—a design to keep an unruly crowd single file. But few people crowded into the station at this hour. This evening would boast more in arrivals and departures.

Rhys answered the ticket master's question. "No thanks. I'm waiting for someone."

This was true, though not entirely. He wouldn't be here when Alice's train arrived from Newcastle, much as he would like to be. His family didn't approve of Alice.

"Mrs. Wright is foolhardy, letting a young lass like Alice run off to Newcastle upon Tyne," his mother had declared.

"But it's for the cause, Mam. No sacrifice is too great for that," Rhys had protested.

"Aye, no sacrifice too great until all the village is dead and gone. You'll not be one of them, you hear me? War will be over soon, and you'll not rush out on its heels and get yourself killed."

He tried to reason with her, but there was no reasoning with fear. And maybe his mam was right to feel that way.

The last time Rhys had seen Alice, she hadn't looked well. Her complexion was sallow, and her countenance changed. Gone was the feisty young woman he'd met at the war bond rally last summer. In her place was a somber, determined woman, single-minded in pursuit of her work at the factory. He still found glimpses of her in the small, stolen moments they cherished in the village and in the letters they squirreled away in the shadowy recess of one of the train station's benches. He held on to those glimpses and the letters.

That was why he had come to the station. He fished in his coat pocket for the note he would leave for Alice. She would receive it hours after he left. He'd be back home tending the livestock by the time her fingers touched the same paper his did now.

"Hey there, lad. Not causing trouble, are you?" The ticket master leaned out from his wooden booth to narrow his eyes at Rhys. "You said you're waiting for someone?"

Rhys shook his head, his fingers still wrapped around the letter in his pocket. "No trouble, sir. I'm meeting them outside. Just came in to get out of the cold for a while."

"Well, warm up and get on then. The station is no place for loitering. Been too many fellows sneaking around here lately with no good reason."

"Aye, sir." Rhys sat on a bench and pretended to busy himself fixing a bootlace. His mind, however, was busy at other tasks. Others were sneaking around? Like who? Did it have something to do with the war? Talk was that the enemy had spies everywhere.

When the ticket master turned to help an arriving traveler, Rhys slid his hand into the crevice between benches where Alice's letter waited. He scooped her note into his pocket before depositing his own in the same space.

The ticket master swiveled his sharp gaze toward Rhys again as he left, but Rhys didn't care. He didn't even mind when the chill sea wind cut through the thin fabric of his coat. All that mattered was the note that Alice—the girl he had grown to care for—had written him.

He distanced himself from the train station before unfolding the paper.

Dear Rhys,

I'm getting used to work at the factory. My days have grown easier as I've grown accustomed to the eccentricities of Canary Girl life.

I do have a worry, though, beyond battles and coastline attacks. A line worker at the factory has been acting suspiciously. He says his name is Henry, and we rode the same train last week, though he doesn't reside in White Church Bay. I have reason to believe his motives are against the crown.

Alice's letter continued with a detailed explanation of her suspicions and ended with her usual signoff. Always, Your Alice

Her words both warmed and chilled Rhys. What was it that the ticket master had said about people skulking around the station? What if he'd been referring to this man, Henry? It was possible he had a sinister design. Spies riddled both city and countryside and made everyone paranoid and distrustful.

What if Henry was something other than a simple line worker? What if Alice became caught in his crosshairs?

Rhys had never felt so helpless, and the feeling stayed with him as he carefully refolded Alice's letter and put it in his coat pocket. He wrapped his hand around it, wishing he could as easily shield her from the danger on their doorstep.

Newcastle upon Tyne
Winter 1917

Rhys's latest letter encouraged Alice to be careful. You don't know if Henry is a danger. Please stay safe. *Didn't he realize that the last few months had stripped her of caution? She was*

a Canary Girl now, serving king and crown. Sacrifices had to be made if the truth was to be found.

They all remained separate on the filling lines. But Henry stayed alone even through the midday meal. While the other factory workers talked and ate together, he sat by himself in a corner of the room used as a makeshift canteen.

"He's an odd duck, all right." Florence followed Alice's gaze. "But what makes you think he's a mole?"

Alice chewed a crust of bread slowly. "The way he studies things, for one. It's as if he's memorizing details." Her gaze fell on a row of posters on the wall. Reminders to be aware that the enemy lurked everywhere, even in this very factory. She scanned the words on the posters.

Listen more than you talk.

Gossip costs lives.

Keep mum with everyone but Mum.

Florence slurped a spoonful of soup. "So? Lots of people observe. That's hardly reason to oust the man as a spy."

Florence might be abrupt, but she wasn't unfair. Alice liked that her friend wasn't given to the automatic prejudice most seemed inclined to. But she also knew her own reasoning went beyond invented paranoia.

"It's not just that. He's also inconsistent. He told Mary that he hailed from Holmfirth. Then he told someone else he grew up in Holmbridge." The two towns were near each other on the map, but they were two altogether different places. How did one forget the name of the place they'd been born?

"Ah, a slip of the tongue, maybe? Or perhaps someone misheard him." Florence appeared unconvinced.

"Maybe." But Alice didn't believe either explanation.

The winter brought increased warfare. The HMS Vanguard *was sunk over Christmas, and with tensions high, Alice feared the worst.*

Henry carried a lighter emblazoned with the Kaiser's language. She'd spotted it on her first day, when it fell from Henry's pocket as he was leaving to catch the train. He was behind her in line that morning—his watery gaze staring right through her—but the guard didn't confiscate his lighter. Henry must have hidden it outside the gates somehow and then retrieved it.

Little matter. When he dropped it, she picked it up. Its outer shell was filled with engraved writing, of which she understood little. The only recognizable word was "einmal." Animal? Or something else? She didn't know what the whole phrase meant, but the simple fact that he carried it made her fearful. It was more than enough to arouse suspicion. Any allegiance with Germany merited watching. She'd handed it back to him with shaking hands. He snatched it without a word and hurried ahead of her for the train.

What if Henry was the enemy in plain sight, feeding information to someone? What if the guard let something slip through the lines and the flick on Henry's contraband lighter was followed by an explosion that destroyed the whole factory and a hundred munitionettes with it?

How could she explain it? On their own, none of her qualms added up to much. But taken together, something was going on. She knew it.

Henry raised his head as if he felt Alice's stare. She immediately dropped her gaze to her plate and dared not look up the rest of the meal.

A supervisor must be told of her suspicions, but she needed more concrete information first. Henry's background. His reasons for traveling to Newcastle upon Tyne. Whether he had family or was truly alone.

All she had now were questions and no answers.

CHAPTER ELEVEN

Soon after sunrise on Sunday morning, Harriet rose to take care of the animals. Then she began getting ready for church. She tried to shove thoughts of the mystery out of her mind. The next step was in Ellie's hands, and all Harriet could do was wait.

After dressing in a warm woolen skirt and a cornflower-blue sweater, she appraised her reflection. Yes, the color suited her nicely. It made her brown hair and eyes appear striking, instead of commonplace.

She smoothed tinted balm onto her lips. Who was she expecting to notice the way she looked? Will? The two of them certainly had a connection, but did it go beyond friendship? What were his true feelings toward her? She wasn't sure she would ever find out.

A sharp shriek pulled Harriet from her reverie."

"Uh, what time does service start again?" Ashley had woken not long after Harriet, but now her voice sounded unusually panicked.

"Nine," Harriet called back. "Why?" She exited the bathroom to find the cause of Ashley's stress.

They still had forty-five minutes until they needed to leave for White Church, but Ashley had had trouble getting Trevor to wake up. She'd joked about him already having a teenager's internal clock. Now Harriet entered his room to find Trevor sitting up in the middle of the bed, his dishwater-blond hair sticking up every which way.

His disheveled hair wasn't the cause of Ashley's concern though. It was the thick wad of pink bubble gum stuck in it above his left ear. Harriet remembered how his evening had been spent enthusiastically chewing through half the box of gumballs Ashley had bought him.

"Trev! Why would you fall sleep with gum in your mouth?" Ashley picked at the sticky glob, but all she succeeded in doing was yanking her son's hair.

"Ouch!" Trevor tried pulling away from her, but she put her hands on his shoulders.

"Hold still. I don't want it to get worse." She turned to Harriet. "What a thing to deal with right before church."

It was a bit of a time crunch, but they could make it. Harriet kept her voice calm and even. "We'll use some peanut butter. Not a problem."

But it was a problem. A quick check of the pantry revealed she had nearly scraped the jar clean yesterday to make Trevor's breakfast.

Ashley wrinkled her nose. "You don't have an extra jar squirreled away somewhere, do you?"

Harriet shook her head. "Sorry. I don't keep extra on hand. It's not as much of a staple here in England as back home."

At that, Ashley looked mildly concerned. "Okay. Do you have anything else that might work? How about ice?"

"Nope, sorry."

"Cola? I've read that can work in a pinch."

Harriet winced. "New Year's resolution—give up soda."

Ashley snapped her fingers. "I've got it. What about mayonnaise?"

"Now that I might have." Harriet ushered Ashley and Trevor into the kitchen, with Trevor protesting all the way.

He tried to wrestle out of his mother's grip. "No way. I don't want to smell like a sandwich."

"It's either this or an impromptu haircut."

Trevor's eyes widened. "What? No way! You're not cutting my hair."

"Okay. Decision made then."

Surprisingly, the mayonnaise treatment did work, though with a lot of protest from Trevor that it smelled horrible. By the time they removed the gum and he'd washed his hair three times and put on nice clothes, it was nearly time for church to start. Even with the short drive, they would probably be late.

Harriet's anticipation at seeing Will was dampened by the potential embarrassment of arriving after the service started. Still, she had committed to attending and knew Aunt Jinny would be disappointed if she skipped.

Societal pressure nipping at her heels, Harriet drove to church. They hurried from the car, and she pulled one of the heavy, wooden double doors open so her group could enter, only to be greeted with the long screech of antique hinges. Everyone—including the pastor—turned to stare at them and their belated arrival.

"Yikes." Harriet sucked a breath of air through her teeth.

A peculiar look crossed Will's face when he saw Harriet. It was such a subtle expression and she was so far away that she couldn't tell what it meant. He was amused? Curious? Or something else entirely?

She directed Ashley and Trevor to an empty seat, trying to be as inconspicuous as possible. Normally, she would have sat in the same pew as her aunt, but she didn't want to cause any more disruption with her entrance than necessary, so they slid into a back pew.

Thankfully, Will didn't seem thrown by their late entrance and began to give the announcements. He reminded the congregants of the upcoming Winter Ladies' Tea, which would take place on Wednesday evening at Aunt Jinny's cottage.

Will finished the announcements and gave the customary greeting that preceded worship. "This is the day the Lord has made. Let us rejoice and be glad in it. Let us stand to worship Him." A collective rustle of movement was followed by the resonant sound of the organ's sonorous tones, filling the room with the strains of "All Things Bright and Beautiful." Afterward, Will resumed his place in the chancel to deliver his message.

Another loud screech of unoiled hinges sounded from the back of the room as he opened his mouth to speak. Harriet swiveled her head around to find the source of the noise, as did most of the people in the congregation. The door swung open, and a rather attractive man walked in.

He wore a neat fisherman's sweater, dress pants, and leather loafers and had the bronze complexion of someone who spent ample time outdoors. He didn't appear as self-conscious about his late arrival as Harriet had. In fact, he was bold enough to catch her eye and grin as he moved up the aisle to the front of the church to sit beside Aunt Jinny.

Ashley nudged Harriet. "My, he makes quite an entrance, doesn't he?"

"I'll say," was all Harriet could manage. How did this stranger know her aunt? The mysterious man acted as though he knew Aunt Jinny as well as Harriet did. Her questions would have to wait until after the service.

Up front, Will began to deliver his message. To her chagrin, Harriet struggled to follow his words. The mysterious man was distracting, and he kept twisting around and looking her way. She was certain she didn't recognize him, yet he seemed to have great familiarity with her family. Her mind was still racing as the service ended and Will gave the closing benediction. Soon, everyone rose from their seats and began filing out of the church.

"Why do I smell mayonnaise?" The crowd obscured Harriet's view of the speaker, but she could tell that the unknown voice had a nasal twang. "Are we having food in the parish hall today?"

Trevor covered his face with his hands and muttered something.

"What was that, kiddo?" Ashley asked.

Trevor removed his hands from his face to reveal a scowl. "I told you using mayo to get the gum out was a bad idea."

"Hey, at least we didn't have to give you a buzz cut," Ashley replied cheerfully.

As Ashley nudged Trevor to exit their row, Harriet got a whiff of tangy mayo mixed with the scent of shampoo. A giggle rose in her throat, and the sensation wasn't helped by the presence of Will, who navigated toward them through the crowds.

"Good morning, Harriet." His warm hazel eyes fixed on her, and her heart fluttered. Goodness, he was handsome. Yet also unreadable. Her earlier mental description of him being akin to a stoic hero in a Jane Austen novel rang true.

"Hi, Will," she replied, glad to hear that her voice didn't tremble.

Will smiled a welcome at Ashley and Trevor. "I see you have some friends with you this morning."

Harriet made the introductions. "This is Ashley Fiske, a good friend of mine from Connecticut. She's visiting with her son, Trevor. It's been so wonderful to catch up with them."

"I can imagine." Will shook Ashley's and Trevor's hands. "It's a pleasure to meet both of you. I hope you enjoyed the service."

"We did," Ashley answered with a smile. "We appreciate the opportunity to worship with your congregation while we're away from home."

"It's a joy to have you here." Will glanced at Harriet again. "What did you think of the sermon?" He watched her carefully, though she couldn't imagine why. Did he care about her opinion that much?

She found herself at a loss for words. She didn't want to admit that she hadn't fully absorbed the message, as she had been distracted by the mysterious man's presence and his reason for sitting with Aunt Jinny. "Um, the sermon was most encouraging."

Will's eyebrows darted upward. "Really? Encouraging?"

"Yes. Quite." How she hoped she'd said the right thing. What was it he'd spoken about again? Hidden truths coming to light? It was something like that, wasn't it?

She wasn't certain, but her answer seemed to please him. Was she imagining it, or did he linger as he shook her hand goodbye?

Ashley's gaze followed Will as he made his way to the vestibule to say goodbye to departing congregants. "I can see why you stay in England," she murmured to Harriet as they filed out of the sanctuary. "Between him and that mysterious hunk making eyes at you earlier..."

Harriet swatted her friend's arm. Then she glanced around to see if anyone else had heard Ashley's comment. "Not so loud." She would be mortified if her feelings for Will were announced in such a public space. As for the new stranger, she would prefer his first impression of her be more than goggling schoolgirl.

Ashley raised her hands. "I'm just saying."

Harriet bit back a laugh. "Hush."

Trevor rushed his mom out of the sanctuary as quickly as possible. "I smell like mayo, Mom!"

Harriet lingered to talk to a few nearby acquaintances.

"Harriet! I wondered where you were." Aunt Jinny embraced her. "Where are Ashley and Trevor?"

"Long story. Headed to the car, I think."

"Oh, I hope everything's all right."

"Small preteen crisis, but Ashley has it well in hand," Harriet assured her.

"I'm glad to hear it. Before you go, I have someone I'd like you to meet." She turned to reveal the handsome stranger who had entered the church after Harriet and her friends. "Harriet, this is Pascal King."

CHAPTER TWELVE

Pascal was as striking up close as he was from afar, and a friendly, earnest expression made him even more attractive. When he grinned at her, the corners of his sparkling blue eyes crinkled appealingly.

Harriet accepted the hand he offered to her to shake, while Aunt Jinny finished introductions. "Pascal, I'd like you to meet my niece, Harriet Bailey. She relocated here from the States last year and took over Dad's vet practice. Harriet, my Dom knew Pascal through his work connections and always spoke highly of him. Pascal is a partner with Paris Legal Alliance."

"But you're so young!" Harriet blurted. "I mean, aren't partners with firms usually older? Like in their fifties?"

Pascal gave a warm chuckle. "I went to university early. So I started working early."

Aunt Jinny took Pascal's arm affectionately. "He's being too modest. Pascal was somewhat of a wunderkind. Very bright and motivated. Finished college before most people begin. He's in town because he's serving as the legal representative for the Evergreen family. They would like the manuscript released to them, and Pascal was sent to ensure that happens. He contacted me yesterday after he made the connection that we were the family who discovered the manuscript. Such a small world, isn't it?"

Any help regarding the manuscript would be welcome. The entire situation had devolved into a complicated mess over the past few days, and Harriet was unsure how to proceed. She was grateful for the legal expertise of someone who seemed competent and already knew her family.

"Your aunt told me that you suspect something of the museum owners," Pascal said with a hint of a French accent. "My clients, Adelaide Evergreen's grandchildren, would be most distressed to hear that."

"I'm not entirely sure." Harriet caught him up to date on what had happened so far, including Robert's involvement and the warning he'd issued to Ellie. She also told him what Ellie uncovered at the museum, about Robert making a forgery. Without that, it would be tempting to assume Harriet had manufactured the entire mystery herself. "I think someone at the museum is hiding something. Something related to the information in chapter eighteen of the manuscript. But I don't have any solid evidence yet."

"And what information would be in this chapter, do you think?"

"I'm not sure," she answered. "Perhaps something relating to black-market activity in the aftermath of the crash? Or more information about the saboteur who caused the crash?"

"Interesting. Very interesting," Pascal murmured.

"Pascal and I spoke briefly when he arrived," Aunt Jinny added. "He believes the Evergreens have a legitimate legal claim regarding ownership of the manuscript. We have several options to pursue."

"Starting with my paying a visit to the museum tomorrow," Pascal said. "You would be surprised how obliging people become when you throw around a few legal terms, and I do think the law is on my clients' side. If that doesn't work, perhaps I could find a legal loophole regarding provenance on your behalf? That is, if you'd like to partner up. We might make faster progress with getting the museum to loosen their death grip on the manuscript if we work together."

Harriet exchanged a glance with Aunt Jinny, who nodded. "We would appreciate any help you could offer."

"Wonderful. I'll contact you right away if I discover anything. And feel free to contact me as well." He withdrew a pen and a stack of business cards from a metal case in his pocket. Then he scribbled something on the back of one of the cards.

His eyes didn't leave Harriet's as he handed her the card. "That's my personal cell number. It's the easiest way to reach me. My firm recently moved into a new office space, and the business number hasn't transferred over yet. Feel free to call me anytime. Day or night."

The sanctuary had mostly emptied by now, so the trio made their way down the aisle and into the vestibule. Will stood at the doors bidding congregants goodbye. At the moment, Chelsea Ward dominated his attention. The woman was a regular at White Church and an ardent admirer of Will. She made no bones about the fact that she would love nothing more than to be a pastor's wife. As Harriet approached the exit, she caught a snippet of their interaction.

Chelsea fluttered her eyelashes at Will. "One thirty still okay to get together?"

Will darted a glance in Harriet's direction. "Yes, I'll see you then. I'm looking forward to it."

"Wonderful." Chelsea practically melted at his side. "I can't tell you how excited I am."

What was that? Harriet's thoughts swirled as she told Will goodbye again and left the church. It certainly sounded like Chelsea had talked Will into a date. What other reason would he have for getting together with her outside of church?

After Harriet parted ways in the parking lot with Pascal and her aunt, Ashley greeted her in the car with raised eyebrows. Her friend immediately teased her as if they were still swoony college girls. "So, have you made a love connection?"

"No, but I have made a connection that might be useful regarding the manuscript." Harriet pushed her key into the ignition and started the car.

Pascal's business card rested in her coat pocket, and Harriet felt more encouraged than she had since the manuscript's discovery. She was confident that with Ellie's help—and now, Pascal's as well—they were one step closer to uncovering the truth behind the train crash.

Harriet had just finished the dinner dishes on Sunday evening when her landline rang. She hurried to the phone and grabbed the receiver. "Hello?"

She wasn't sure what she expected on the other end of the line, but it certainly wasn't the silence she received.

"Hello?" she asked again. Still no answer, so she hung up. *Must have been a wrong number.* She consoled herself with the idea, though visions of the shadowy figure she'd seen outside her aunt's cottage still lingered in her mind.

She set the phone in its cradle only to have it ring again. She jumped before she could stop herself.

"Hello?" This time she pushed out the word with more force. "Anyone there?"

"Hello, Harriet? It's Van. Could I bother you for a moment?"

"Yes, of course. What can I do for you?"

The detective constable cleared his throat. "I wanted to ask you about Polly. Is she upset with me? I know you two spend a lot of time together, and I thought she might have mentioned it."

Harriet was hesitant to divulge information, but wasn't this the opportunity Polly had asked her to take advantage of? "She's not upset. I can assure you of that."

"But she is avoiding me. Do you know why, and if you do, can you tell me?"

"I think she feels as though *you* might be upset. That you're unhappy in the relationship."

"Unhappy? Where would she get that idea?" Van sounded genuinely puzzled.

"She feels that you've been distracted lately. It has her worried." Harriet swallowed. The less she said, the better. She had read enough books to know that being an intermediary didn't often end well. Economy of words was the way to go. "I think Polly would prefer that you be completely transparent with her about your feelings. Does that make sense?"

"I think so. I need to talk to her about how I'm feeling. Reassure her about our relationship."

"Precisely."

"I understand," Van said. "Thank you for your help, Harriet."

"Of course."

Satisfied that she had smoothed things over between her friends, Harriet hung up the phone, only to have it ring once more. She was certainly popular tonight.

She picked it up hesitantly. "Hello?"

"Hello, Harriet? This is Ellie Caldwell. I'm at the museum." The doctoral student's voice sounded weary. No wonder, given the long hours she'd been putting in with the internship and her studies.

"Ellie." Harriet let her breath rush out in a whoosh of relief. "Did you find the missing chapter?"

A rustling of papers preceded Ellie's answer. "I did. And I found something that implicates a family by the surname of Miller."

"Miller?" That was awfully close to an Anglicized version of Müeller. Too close for comfort, actually. "Is there anything else you can tell me? What about Robert? How do you think he's involved?"

"Get this." Ellie sounded triumphant. "I found proof. Actual proof that they're using his abilities to create a fake copy of chapter eighteen—"

Harriet could hear more noises in the background of Ellie's call. A door opening? Followed by slight murmuring that sounded like someone talking to her? A flicker of suspicion rose in Harriet. It was Sunday evening. The museum was closed. Why did it sound like there was someone else there?

"Is someone there with you?" she asked.

"N-no. You must be hearing people walking by outside." But Harriet didn't buy it. Ellie's voice trembled.

"All right." Harriet tried to keep her voice level. But she could tell something was wrong. Otherwise, why would Ellie's tone have changed so quickly? "Continue what you were saying. The chapter had something to do with the Miller family?"

"Uh, no. I was mistaken," Ellie replied.

"Mistaken about what?"

"I—I misread the text. The chapter didn't say anything negative about the Miller family. The Millers helped the village in the aftermath of the crash, donating time and resources to the repair efforts. Henry Barnett, also known as Hans Goebel, is named as a person of interest, however. Adelaide thought Goebel was the one who caused the train crash."

Neither the name Henry nor Hans rang a bell, so Harriet made a mental note to research them.

Ellie continued. "Another person of note is a Rhys Bailey. He profited from the wreck by selling damaged cargo goods on the black market in the months to follow."

That last name came as a huge blow. Rhys was her great-great-granduncle. Aunt Jinny said he might have had something to do with the crash, but Harriet couldn't wrap her mind around the idea that he'd been involved in a nefarious way.

Harriet sank into a nearby armchair. She wasn't sure what to say. Suspicion flickered, but she didn't want to believe someone had gotten to Ellie. The doctoral student was so helpful. She'd gone out of her way to help Harriet, and Harriet had come to see her as a friend. "Rhys Bailey is my relative."

Ellie sounded startled. "Oh no. Harriet, I had no idea. I'm so sorry."

"You're certain you have the original chapter and that's what it says? Rhys Bailey profited from the accident?"

"I'm sorry, Harriet." This time Ellie sounded resolute. "I'm looking at the original. It's right here, in black and white."

What a mess. Either Ellie wasn't telling the truth, which Harriet didn't want to consider, or Harriet knew less about her family than she had thought. Both scenarios were unwelcome. "I almost wish—no, that's silly."

"What?"

"I was going to say that I almost wish we hadn't taken the manuscript to the museum in the first place. If I could do it over, I don't know if I'd support it going public." The entire situation had become less of a boon and more of a bother.

"Surely you don't mean that," Ellie protested. "It's a piece of White Church Bay history, and an important one at that. I know it's unexpected to have one of your relatives named, but it can't be that bad. Over a hundred years ago should make it water under the bridge, right?"

Harriet didn't know who Ellie was trying to convince more—Harriet or herself. She did her best to shake off the negative emotions Ellie's information had raised. "Never mind. What does the chapter say?"

"The book references a railway employee who gave an eyewitness testimony that he saw Rhys Bailey lingering by the tracks the day before the accident. The footnotes specifically reference incident logs from December 1, 1917."

It couldn't be true. The information didn't square with anything Harriet knew of her family, or their reputation around here. "That doesn't make any sense. You're sure he's the one named in the chapter?"

"Positive." Ellie sounded truly remorseful. "I'm so sorry, Harriet. I also wanted you to know that I, um, need to pause my internship. I'm afraid I've overextended myself. I don't know that I'm going to be working for the museum anymore, but if you stop by tomorrow morning, I'm sure someone can get you a copy of the chapter."

Harriet finished her phone call with Ellie and hung up in disbelief. She should fill Aunt Jinny in on this new development, but she couldn't bring herself to do it. It couldn't be true. She came from a long line of upright men and women who had proved to be on the right side of history. Rhys just couldn't have been any different.

Yet a small sliver of doubt started to work its way into her heart. Was she only seeing what she wanted to see? She had to find out more information. How did Adelaide Evergreen know Rhys Bailey in the first place? And why had the manuscript been abandoned? Could Rhys have hidden it to protect his reputation?

Still sitting, she sent a prayer heavenward. *Dear Lord, please let Ellie be mistaken. Please help me clear my family's name.*

She knew she should be praying for the truth to be revealed whether she liked it or not, but she couldn't bring herself to. What did it say about her view of the world if her own family member was the villain in a historical tragedy?

She didn't want to consider it. So she pushed Rhys's possible involvement to the back of her mind. The suspicion that hung over the rest of the phone call was another matter entirely, however.

Harriet had thought she'd heard someone else at the museum, so why had Ellie insisted she was alone? And why the sudden announcement that she was leaving her internship, which was so important to her? Not to mention that the new information in the chapter didn't make sense with anything Ellie had told Harriet previously.

Harriet rose from her armchair. Despite the maelstrom of questions swirling in her mind, she knew one thing. It was time for her to stop reacting and take charge. She could chase rabbit trails all day long and get nowhere, or she could find some answers. The real questions she needed to explore surrounding the manuscript lay beneath the surface. But how to uncover them?

CHAPTER THIRTEEN

Newcastle upon Tyne
Winter 1917

Alice decided her next step would be to engage Henry in conversation. If she could get him to talk more, maybe she could discover where his allegiance lay.

When her shift ended at the factory, she changed as usual but lingered to button her coat. Soon, Henry crossed her path. She pretended their meeting was coincidental.

"Henry!" she called after him as he headed for the exit.

He didn't turn around, only pulled a mud-colored cap low over his eyes. Perhaps he hadn't heard her.

She called his name again. A small, almost imperceptible turn of his head told her he was aware of her presence. She ran across the expanse of scrubby grass that encircled the factory and caught him by the arm as if they were friends.

He jerked away as though her touch were a fire that burned him. "What do you want from me?" His tone was gruff, his voice low. "I've seen you watching me."

"I don't want anything from you." Alice's heart pounded, but she tried to keep her words light. "I noticed you were sitting by yourself. I thought I would introduce myself in case you haven't met many people yet. I'm Alice Wright. And you're Henry, but I'm afraid I haven't caught your last name."

Henry angled his hat to shield his eyes even more. "Barnett. A good English name, though I haven't lived here all my life. Satisfied?"

"Virginia mentioned you were from Holmbridge. Is that right? I believe I have some family there. What part of town did you live in?"

He glared at her but didn't reply.

She pivoted to another tactic. "I'm sorry, you must think I'm incredibly nosy. I prattle on so when I get nervous. What did you do before you came here? Were you a farmer?"

She wanted to root out his past. If he talked more, she'd be able to spot any inconsistencies in his story.

"I wasn't a farmer."

"Oh, I thought maybe you worked outdoors. Your skin is darkened by the sun." His copper complexion was a different shade than exposure to chemicals at the factory produced.

He stopped in his tracks and turned to face her full-on, making her wonder if she'd hit a nerve. His watery blue eyes bore into hers as if he was trying to read her secrets, not the other way around. Was he on to her? Did he suspect why she was so interested in the details of his life?

She forced a laugh. "My, so serious. I'm trying to be friendly."

"The dying aren't the type to make friends. Leave me be." Without another word, Henry pivoted and walked away from her. He was a tall man, and the length of his strides quickly carried him out of sight.

The dying? That shook her. She took advantage of the distance he'd placed between them, as well as the gathering darkness, to follow him. He got on the train and got off at Whitby.

Sticking to the shadows, Alice trailed him to a common boardinghouse. When he entered the building, she sneaked forward to peer through a window. What she saw, however, surprised her.

The man took off his hat and coat and set them aside. Then he took off his shoes and peeled his socks off his feet. For propriety's sake, Alice started to turn away. But before she did, she saw Henry stand to cross the room barefoot to a washbasin. He filled the basin with water and dunked his socks inside.

He's doing laundry. *The disappointed thought sprang to Alice's mind. Shouldn't she be glad the man was an ordinary sort, without ill intent?*

Her disappointment didn't last long, as it soon became clear that Henry was not doing laundry.

She watched in shock as he pulled the socks from the dingy water and wrung them out over another bowl. Then he opened a valise on the desk and removed a sheaf of paper, a small glass bottle, and a fountain pen.

He slowly poured the water he had squeezed from the socks into the small bottle. The liquid was dark, nearly the color of black treacle. Then he dipped the tip of the pen in the liquid and began to scratch words across the paper.

Alice needed to get a better view of things. She leaned closer as the wind picked up, and a branch from a nearby tree smacked the glass. Henry's head snapped toward the window.

Alice ducked out of sight just in time—she hoped. Her heart thudded even harder in her chest than when Henry and she had talked.

Things were getting infinitely more complicated. It was obvious he was up to something, but what? Was he truly dying? Did the man have even less to lose than Alice had originally thought? No family. No friends. Maybe not even a future.

Worried thoughts chased each other. She had to know what was in the letter. She needed to know if he was planning some kind of sabotage at the factory or leaking information to the enemy. She wished again that Rhys was with her. She felt as alone and uncertain as she had that first day in Newcastle upon Tyne.

What was she to do next? She longed for someone to guide her along the right path.

Monday morning dawned cold and bright. Harriet didn't have any early appointments, so she left the clinic in Polly's hands and headed into town. Fisherman's Lane Museum was officially slated to reopen to the public today, and Harriet needed to see for herself that Ellie was gone. Surely she hadn't left town already. Last night's conversation with the doctoral student left Harriet with a multitude of questions.

Harriet drove the Beast to the usual lot and parked. Aha! Ellie's distinctive canary-yellow Volkswagen was there. Maybe Harriet hadn't missed her after all. She hurried into the village.

The museum door was unlocked when she arrived. She opened the door and braced herself to face Petra. But the stern-faced woman wasn't sitting at the front desk. In fact, the main room of the museum was empty.

"Hello?" Harriet called. She took a few steps past the desk to peer into the back room. But there was no answer.

Ellie must be here. Her only inside ally couldn't have disappeared so quickly. Inching into the hallway, Harriet caught a glimpse of the room that must be Robert's workspace. A hulking antique typewriter took up half the desk, the rest of which was covered with scattered papers and a random assortment of items. If she could just see the papers…

Silence made her bold. She situated her bag on her shoulder before crossing the hallway and entering the room. She could see the items on the desk more clearly now. A jar of muddy water. Tubes of paint, yellow ochre and burnt sienna. A hairdryer. Something that resembled a seam ripper. And there were two piles of paper. One seemed to be the original manuscript. The other was a work in progress of one of the chapters, some pages white and pristine, others dyed and tattered to mimic age.

Ellie had been right. Robert was forging a copy of the document. Harriet started to pick up the fake pages to study them more closely.

"What are you doing here? This area is off-limits."

Harriet jumped, knocking papers off the desk, and spun around to find Robert in the doorway. His arms were folded tightly across his chest, and his expression was disapproving.

She bent to retrieve the papers, but he stopped her. "Leave them. What are you doing back here?"

"I'm sorry. I was searching for Ellie."

"And you thought you'd find her in my private office?"

"No, I was—"

"What do you need from Ellie?"

Harriet decided to take the honest route. "I've been communicating with her about the missing chapter. She's been helping me."

Robert raised an eyebrow. "She should have been focusing on work. Not on an outside task she wasn't assigned."

Harriet hurried to paint Ellie in a positive light. "She didn't take time away from her work. She was generous enough to help me outside of work hours."

"Outside of work hours?"

Harriet realized she'd said too much. No one knew that Ellie was at the museum last night. Other than the person who had been in the background of her call.

Robert laughed, but it didn't sound at all pleasant. "Don't look so startled. I know Ellie was here last night."

So Ellie lied. There had been someone at the museum with her, and it must have been Robert. Had he threatened her again? Was he blackmailing her so she would remain quiet about the manuscript's possible tie to the Müeller family?

Robert continued. "Ellie's not the only one who can work overtime. Though, in her case, she may have pushed herself too far."

"What do you mean?"

"She's overworked. That's why we sent her home. She's been burning the candle at both ends for too long, and she finally snapped. Spinning all kinds of paranoid stories. She needs to take a break."

Ellie hadn't been paranoid. She hadn't imagined Robert's threats or the missing chapter. Harriet was certain of it. And what did he mean, they sent her home? Had Ellie left White Church Bay, even though her vehicle was still here?

Harriet lifted her chin. "All I want is the chapter. You can understand why I feel like I'm getting the runaround. It feels to me like someone's trying to hide something."

"I understand. But that's all been a misunderstanding. Chalk it up to the ravings of a sleep-deprived doctoral student. You must have noticed how overworked Ellie was."

Harriet thought back to her few interactions with Ellie. She hated to admit it, but she could see Robert's point. On their first meeting, hadn't Ellie's arms been weighed down with papers to cart home so she could keep working? Hadn't she been overly eager to help Harriet outside of work hours? And that day in the shop when Ashley picked up toothpaste, Ellie looked as if she had pulled an all-nighter the evening before.

"Don't worry." Robert sounded like the voice of calm reason. "We'll get things taken care of. In fact, I made a copy of the chapter for you myself."

Robert pushed past Harriet to get to his desk, where he retrieved a stack of copied pages. He showed them to her, and she scanned the first few paragraphs of the elusive chapter eighteen.

Robert peered over her shoulder. "It's quite fascinating, to be working for the Müellers when their ancestors are named in this book. A real full-circle moment, wouldn't you say? The Millers created the history that the Müellers now protect."

Quite fascinating, indeed. But had history been rewritten? Or was Harriet staring at the truth in black and white? She could only hope she wasn't, because the chapter confirmed what Ellie had told her.

Rhys Bailey was guilty.

"What about the information Ellie gave me? That the Millers were somehow involved with the crash? What evidence is there to prove Rhys Bailey did anything wrong?"

"Right there. Don't you see?" Robert pointed at a line in the text. "A confirmed eyewitness account of him at the tracks around the time of the crash. Station logs confirm the same thing. It says his behavior was 'suspicious.'"

"It can't be true. I'm descended from his brother. I would've heard stories passed down over the years."

Robert gave a condescending smile. "Who wants to admit to skeletons in the closet? Look how upset it's made you. But don't take my word for it. History's out there for the researching."

He refused to say anything more, leaving her with little option but to leave the museum in an even worse state of mind than when she had arrived.

The yellow Volkswagen was gone from the parking lot when Harriet reached her Land Rover. Harriet fumbled in her purse for her cell phone and called Ellie.

"Come on. Please answer." She whispered the words as the line rang.

Just when she was ready to give up, Ellie answered. "Hello?" The doctoral student sounded exhausted.

"Ellie? This is Harriet Bailey. I need to talk to you."

"Oh, Harriet. Now's not a great time. I'm traveling back to York right now."

"Please? I know something's going on with the manuscript. Something you're not telling me."

"Harriet, I really can't do this."

"Is it Robert? Is he blackmailing you so you'll keep quiet about what you know? You can tell me the truth."

Ellie sighed. "The truth can be complicated. Listen, I can't tell you everything right now, but please trust me. I was wrong about Robert. He has a good side. I thought he was greedy and self-serving, but he's not."

Harriet kept her guard up. She would love nothing more than to trust Ellie, but who knew what was really going on? "What made you change your opinion of Robert?"

"The university has had some budget cuts in recent years, and they've hit Robert's department the hardest. He's been pinching pennies and funneling every spare pound into his work there."

That was news. Ellie's information did soften Harriet's assessment of Robert. He might be a more complex person than she'd originally given him credit for, but did that mean he wasn't doing something unethical? He had threatened Ellie and misled Harriet, and now he had an even clearer motive than simple greed if there was money to be made from the Evergreen manuscript.

Things were always trickier when one's job was on the line.

CHAPTER FOURTEEN

Harriet fought distraction the rest of the day at the clinic. Robert had planted a seed of doubt in her mind. Ellie was overworked, that was true. Harriet had heard the exhaustion in her voice. Add to that the worrisome fact that some of the evidence Robert referenced did point to Rhys's guilt, but she wouldn't be satisfied until she knew for certain. She was wrapping up work for the day when the clinic's landline rang.

Since Polly was in the back cleaning out crates, Harriet picked up the phone. "Cobble Hill Veterinary Clinic. How may I help you?"

A man with a thick Irish brogue greeted her. "Hello? Is Doc Bailey about?"

"Yes, this is Harriet Bailey."

"No, no. I mean the gentleman."

"Dr. Harold Bailey, my grandfather, passed away last year and left the clinic to me. I'm Dr. Harriet Bailey."

The man's voice softened. "I'm sorry to hear that. I knew your grandad some years ago when my family and I lived in White Church Bay. He helped us out many a time. My wife and I just retired here and have a small hobby farm outside of town. My name's Finn O'Malley."

"Welcome back to White Church Bay, Mr. O'Malley. May I ask what animals you and your wife raise?"

"You can call me Finn, Doc. We're non-traditionists, I guess you could call us." Finn suddenly sounded hesitant. "We raise birds."

"Chickens?"

"No."

"Turkeys? Pheasants? Guineas? Am I getting warm?"

"Not quite." He cleared his throat. "We raise emus."

"How novel." But why be so secretive about that?

"So you don't have anything against working with them then?" Hope buoyed Finn's voice.

"No, I don't think so. Is there a particular reason you ask?"

"My wife and I find that emus get a bad rap. Some people think they're too aggressive, and I admit, we're still working on getting ours socialized and settled in. They can be a little dodgy."

Well, a difficult animal or two was nothing she couldn't handle. She'd dealt with some tricky situations before, and everything always worked out.

"It doesn't bother me," she replied in answer to Finn's worries. "What do you need done?"

"That's absolutely brilliant. The mob needs some kind of treatment. Parasites, I think? They're picking their feathers clean out." *Mob* was the term for a group of emus.

"I can take care of that." Harriet gathered the necessary information and blocked out time in her schedule to visit Finn's farm the following morning.

She hung up and started to retrieve her coat and keys when the phone rang again.

By this time, Polly had made her way back to the desk and beat Harriet to the receiver. "Hello?" Then a pause. "Hello? Is there anyone there?" She shrugged and hung up. "Another one of those buggy calls where they don't speak. Whoever it is has a dog."

Polly didn't seem particularly worried about the call, but it unsettled Harriet. Given all the difficulty surrounding the manuscript, she wasn't as likely to believe it was a wrong number as she once had.

Spurred on by the mysterious caller and all that had happened, Harriet was even more eager to push forward on the manuscript mystery. As soon as she freshened up at home, she invited Ashley and Trevor to visit the local public library with her. "It's time for a research trip. I need to find more information about the S&W Railway crash and about Adelaide Evergreen."

Trevor's eyes lit up. "A library? And stuff about trains? Count me in."

"Sure," Ashley agreed. "Let me grab my coat."

It didn't take long to get into town. The library smelled pleasantly of glue and aged paper. Trevor quickly located the section he was interested in and disappeared among the stacks. Ashley and Harriet headed to the nearby genealogy section to search for information.

"I can't believe how much Trevor has grown up in the past year," Harriet said. "The last time I saw him, all he would talk about was cartoons. He didn't seem interested in reading at all. These days, he's quite a bookworm."

Ashley shook her head. "I know. A year is a lifetime in the world of a child. Trevor has changed a lot since—well, you know. That's really when he became so interested in books. It's been a tough year for him. I'm grateful he's coping as well as he is."

Harriet put a hand on her friend's arm. "How about you? How are you doing?"

Ashley leveraged a sigh. "I'm fine. Just struggling to find my way, I guess."

"If you need anything, I'm here for you. You know that, right?"

"I do." Ashley set her lips in a tight line. "But I don't want to talk about it. Okay?"

Harriet nodded. Though she hated to abandon the subject, she would respect Ashley's wishes. "Why don't we divide and conquer with research? I think we'll cover more ground that way."

Ashley agreed and volunteered to search through genealogy databases for information on the specific people mentioned in the manuscript while Harriet tried to find information on the train crash and Adelaide Evergreen.

Harriet logged into a computer to search the public access catalog for books and was pleased to discover the library had a decent collection referencing Evergreen and the S&W Railway crash.

She ventured down the stacks to locate the section the books were supposed to be in, only to be met with a gaping space on the shelf.

She checked the scrap of paper on which she had scribbled identifying information. The call numbers she'd written were correct. The database said the books were available. Yet nothing was on the shelf. It was too much of a coincidence for Harriet's comfort. Was the empty shelf purposeful? Had Robert or the Müellers been here before her and cleared out the books? Or perhaps someone else?

She located the front desk librarian. "The books I need aren't on the shelf, but the catalog says they should be. Can you help me?"

The librarian adjusted her glasses and stood from her seat. "Certainly. May I see your list?"

Harriet handed her the list of call numbers.

The librarian studied her writing with pursed lips. "Ah, I believe all these books were checked out a few minutes ago by a patron."

"Someone checked out *all* the books on the S&W Railway crash?" Whoever had done it was thorough. The list contained at least ten titles. "I don't suppose you could tell me who, could you? I need some information that might be in those books."

The librarian shook her head. "Patron confidentiality. I can try to help you find some online information on your topic if you'd like."

With the librarian's assistance, Harriet printed a few pages with information about Adelaide Evergreen and Hans Goebel, including their obituaries. It wasn't much, but it was better than nothing. Feeling defeated, she headed back to the genealogy area, where Ashley was busy making copies.

"Find anything?" Harriet asked.

"Not much. I thought there would be more information, but the microfilm roll I needed was missing from the drawer. Odd, huh?"

Not so odd after the empty shelf Harriet had encountered. She remembered what Ellie told her about the conversation between Petra and Garrison. Ellie had said Petra was intent on erasing the history of the crash. Was that why the collection on the S&W Railway crash had been cleared out?

Ashley continued. "I was able to track the Müeller line back to the Millers, which isn't a huge surprise, but it was a good piece of information to confirm."

"Good work," Harriet told her friend.

Ashley gathered Trevor, and together the three of them made their way to the front of the library to pay for their printouts. Harriet was frustrated, but what more could they do? Every path they went down about the manuscript led to a dead end. The scraps of information they'd found would have to tide them over until she could figure out her next steps.

Harriet returned home to find a strange car idling outside. As soon as she parked, the driver's door of the unfamiliar car opened, and a man got out. It was Robert Callum.

Harriet felt a little spooked, so she rolled her window down only a few inches. "Robert, what are you doing here?"

To his credit, Robert kept a respectable distance and held up his hands to show no ill intent. "I tried to call your landline, but no one answered. I need to talk to Pascal King, and I think I have the wrong phone number. I know you've been communicating with him, so I was wondering if you could give me the correct number."

Was that all? "It's late, Robert. Isn't that something that could wait until tomorrow?"

"I'm afraid not. I need to speak with him immediately."

The last thing Harriet wanted was to make life easier for Robert. He certainly hadn't helped her. But maybe he would leave her alone if she gave him the number.

"All right. Let me find it." She fished in her purse for the business card Pascal had given her and read him the number embossed on its front. It didn't feel appropriate to give him the lawyer's personal cell phone number scribbled on the back.

Instead of writing down the number, Robert punched the digits into his cell phone to place a call. Then he held the phone to his ear. Harriet started to say something, but he held up a finger to silence her.

Did he really expect her to wait while he conducted business? This was her personal property, and she would prefer if he left so she could enter her home in peace. A flicker of frustration worked through her, and she shrugged apologetically at Ashley.

Something must have gone wrong with Robert's call, because he soon removed the phone from his ear and stared at the screen. He looked as irritated as Harriet felt.

"Are you positive you gave me the right number?" he asked.

"I'm sure." She read him the number again.

He confirmed that it was the one he had tried to call then clenched his fists in anger. "What is this? A joke? The number isn't in service. I have to get in touch with Mr. King immediately. Does he have another number?"

Harriet bit her lip. She remembered now that Pascal was in a new office space and the number was still being transferred, but she wasn't sure if it was her place to share that information.

"Well?" Robert tapped his foot impatiently. "Time is money. Does Mr. King have another number?"

Harriet wasn't Pascal's secretary. And Robert hadn't been particularly accommodating of her questions. But her last conversation with Ellie played in her mind. What if things weren't as they seemed?

"I have another number that I can try for him." She retrieved her phone and punched in the numbers.

Thankfully, Pascal's personal number worked, and Robert appeared satisfied. She passed the phone to him after greeting Pascal. Robert chatted briefly with the lawyer and mentioned something about arranging a private meeting before ending the call and handing the phone back to Harriet. Then he got in his car and drove off without so much as a thank-you.

"What was that about?" Ashley asked as Robert's taillights faded into the distance.

"I don't know."

The situation was curious and stoked the fire of suspicion against Robert that Harriet had already been tending.

CHAPTER FIFTEEN

As Harriet wrapped up her evening chores at home, she pushed away worries over Robert's sudden appearance on her property and tried to refocus on the mystery.

The library had been a bust. One measly book about Adelaide Evergreen that didn't even mention the crash. Harriet had skimmed half of it already, and she hadn't found any information that cleared up anything. She needed to explore other avenues but wasn't sure where to start.

She picked up the phone and called someone she trusted to give her perspective.

Will's familiar voice came over the line. "Hello?"

"Hi, Will. It's Harriet. Is this a good time to talk?"

"Certainly. What's on your mind?"

"I need some advice."

"I'm happy to help any way I can. Is this something to do with the Adelaide Evergreen manuscript that was found at your aunt's cottage? Jinny told me about it at church."

Harriet sighed, relieved that she didn't have to fill him in on the details. "Yes. Just when I think I'm onto something, I hit a brick wall. Ellie Caldwell, who works at the museum, was trying to help me figure out what's going on with the missing chapter. But then she suddenly started acting evasive. You work with people for a living. How do you know when they're telling the truth?"

Will hummed in thought. "That's a complex question. I don't know a foolproof way to ascertain honesty. But I have learned one thing throughout the years that has helped me."

"What's that?"

"'For there is nothing hidden that will not be disclosed, and nothing concealed that will not be known or brought out into the open.'"

How like a pastor, to answer her question with Scripture.

"That's from Luke, right?"

"Yes." Will sounded pleased. "Remember that the truth is often buried in a shallow grave. It doesn't change with circumstances or time, and it doesn't take as much to dig it up as one would think."

"That gives me a more hopeful outlook. Thank you."

"Of course. Anything else you need?"

"No, that's perfect for right now." She told him goodbye and ended the phone call.

Maybe she needed to know more about her family history before she wrote off a relative. Since the manuscript had been found at the dower cottage, perhaps some other belongings of Rhys's were there as well.

It was drawing close to bedtime, but a quick call confirmed that Aunt Jinny was still awake. Harriet caught her aunt up to speed with the mystery's recent developments, trying to downplay the implication that Rhys might have been involved in the crash. No sense worrying her aunt until she had more solid information.

"Do you think we could search your attic?" Harriet asked. "We promise not to stay too late."

"Of course. Come on over. I'll put the kettle on."

Ashley and Trevor accompanied Harriet to her aunt's house, and the group searched the attic for a good half hour. However, their efforts revealed nothing more substantial than a few dust bunnies.

"Boy, I could go for some of that pie from the other day." Trevor looked wistful. Apparently, searching had worked up an appetite for the ten-year-old.

Aunt Jinny laughed. "I think I might have a couple of pieces left, if it's okay with your mum."

"Fine by me," Ashley answered. "I've been dreaming about that pie ever since my last bite. It's delicious."

"It's in the fridge. Go ahead and help yourselves."

Murmuring appreciation, Ashley and Trevor headed for the kitchen, leaving Harriet and her aunt alone in the attic. Aunt Jinny hefted a cardboard box to her chest. "This one looks promising. Let's take it downstairs."

When they got to the sitting room, Aunt Jinny placed the box on the floor before giving Harriet a knowing smile. "You know, Pascal asked about you after you left church yesterday. He seemed quite interested."

Heat rushed to Harriet's face, but she hoped her aunt didn't notice. She dove for the contents of the box in an effort to hide her reaction. "Oh? What did he say?"

"Just that he enjoyed talking with you." Aunt Jinny raised her eyebrows. "He said that you two seemed to get along well."

"I enjoyed meeting him." As much as Aunt Jinny might be trying to play matchmaker, a certain someone else hovered on the edges of Harriet's mind. Yet would it really hurt anything to get to know

Pascal better? It was probably silly not to, since she wasn't sure where she stood with Will and she thought he might be dating around.

Aunt Jinny took a pile of papers from the box. "I mentioned that you weren't seriously involved with anyone. I hope you don't mind."

"What?" Harriet suddenly got a taste of how Polly felt. She had met Pascal once the day before. Was she ready for a date with him? The whole process felt too sudden. It also felt a little awkward to know her aunt was talking about her relationship status to this man Harriet didn't know. Especially with how much Aunt Jinny had been nudging her toward Will since she'd moved to town.

Did Aunt Jinny know something about how Will felt that Harriet didn't, and now she was trying to shuffle Harriet off on someone else before she got hurt?

"Don't worry," Aunt Jinny reassured her. "There's no pressure. I just think it's nice for you to meet other people your age. Pascal was an impressive young attorney, according to your uncle. A lot of water has passed under the bridge since then, but I think Pascal could be a good person to know. He's really going to be able to help with the manuscript."

Trevor and Ashley must have finished their pie, because after a clattering of dishes in the sink, they reentered the sitting room.

"You two look like the cats that swallowed the canaries." Ashley raised her eyebrows at Aunt Jinny and Harriet. "What have you been talking about?"

"Just girl talk," was Aunt Jinny's answer.

Trevor started to make a face but yawned instead.

Ashley laughed. "I think someone needs to hit the hay. Are we done searching for tonight?"

"Wait." Aunt Jinny set her teacup onto its saucer and rose from her seat. "I have one more place I'd like to check. Give me a minute."

She excused herself from the group and was gone for a while before returning to the room. She was covered in dust and clutched a small cardboard box to her chest. "I almost forgot about the guest room. There's storage underneath the bed, and that's where I found this box. There are letters inside, but there's got to be something else in here as well. It's too heavy for only letters."

Aunt Jinny set the box on the coffee table, and Harriet took a deep breath before opening it. The box was full of snapshots, greeting cards, and letters from different decades. It was too much to go through at such a late hour, so she set them aside to study later. When she got to the bottom of the box, her hand brushed against something rough.

She pulled out the rest of the photos and correspondence so she could see what the box held. She carefully removed a couple of small nails and something that looked like an oversized rusty version of them. "What is this?"

Trevor had been slumped sleepily against Ashley on the sofa, but when he saw what Harriet held, he sat upright, his eyes brightening. "Whoa, cool. It's an old railroad spike."

Harriet remembered how he had excitedly chattered on about the Central Pacific Railroad's golden spike the day they'd gone to the museum. So this spike had connected rails to track at some point? She turned it over in her hands.

Trevor leaned over Harriet's shoulder and gave an approving whistle. "I bet it's over a hundred years old."

"How do you know how old it is?" Ashley asked.

"Because of the number on the date nails," Trevor explained.

He pointed to an obscure marking on the head of one of the small nails. It had completely escaped Harriet's attention, but now, she could see a faint number—*16*—stamped on the flat surface of the nailhead.

"That's the year the railroad ties were treated," Trevor continued. "That's how they kept track."

Aunt Jinny took the pieces from Harriet, her features contorted with worry. "Why are these with our family's belongings? Is it possible—" She broke off and put her hand over her mouth.

Harriet finished Aunt Jinny's thought. "Is it possible that these have a connection to the S&W Railway crash?" She shivered. "Could it be possible that Rhys was involved in the crash? I can't think of another reason for these to be included in our family belongings."

"I don't know, love." Aunt Jinny's voice was soft.

"No. No way." Ashley was adamant. "Trevor saw a different version of chapter eighteen. And from what you said, Ellie mentioned it too. There's some narrative that might not involve your relative. Some version of history that implicates the Müellers. Your family is innocent, Harriet. I know it."

Harriet sighed. "I'd love it if you were right. But how on earth do we prove it?"

"I don't know. I guess we keep exploring the paths in front of us," Ashley said.

"'A man plans his steps, but the Lord directs his paths,'" Aunt Jinny reminded them.

But where was He directing them? That was the question. "We need to find out if these items—the spike and nails—match the ones the S&W Railway used," Harriet said.

"It's worth a check." Ashley furrowed her brow. "But how do we find that out?"

"We go to the location of the crash." Harriet opened her laptop and conducted a quick search online. "And apparently, we'll be retracing our steps. The station is at the parking lot across from the Windsor Hotel. We need to visit the Cinder Track."

CHAPTER SIXTEEN

What's the Cinder Track?" Trevor asked eagerly.

"It's the route of a defunct railroad line that runs from Scarborough through White Church Bay to Whitby," Aunt Jinny explained. "Today, hikers and bikers use the path. Some of the track is still in excellent shape, even though the lines closed in the 1960s, and many of the station buildings have been preserved and are available for visitors to explore."

"One of the station buildings now serves as a museum of information about the line," Harriet added. "I've visited it before, but I don't remember the exhibits very well. Given Trevor's interest in trains, I had planned to take you guys there anyway. Perhaps we could find some information that would verify the date nails and the spike."

"A spectacular idea," Aunt Jinny said. Then she yawned. "Forgive me. It's past my bedtime."

"We'll get out of your hair then. Thanks for everything," Harriet said, rising.

"It's a shame we didn't find the date nails earlier today," Ashley said as they left Aunt Jinny's cottage and navigated through the dark to Harriet's home. "You have work tomorrow. Maybe Trevor and I can figure out a way to get to the track on our own and check things out."

"No need for that," Harriet replied. She clutched the cardboard box to her chest that contained all the various paper ephemera they had found at the cottage. "I have an appointment scheduled in the morning at a farm not far from there. We can swing by on our way back home."

Harriet stayed up far too late that night, going through the box. Included among the items was a thick bundle of notes addressed to Rhys from a woman named Alice Wright. The name didn't ring a bell with Harriet.

Had Alice been Rhys's girlfriend? Though Harriet didn't have the benefit of seeing the letters Rhys had sent Alice, Alice's notes overflowed with sentiment. Not only did she speak of her devotion to Rhys, but she also spoke of what seemed to be their common commitment to their country.

As Alice's letters progressed, however, there was less mention of romance and more of her worries over spy activity at the munitions plant where she worked. In the final letter, Alice revealed her plan to shadow a man she believed to be working for the Central Powers. But that was where the letters stopped.

A search of her own home's attic—where she'd found plenty of family mementos before—revealed an engraved wooden box. Harriet opened the lid to reveal a collection of medals. A note on the box's velvet lining under the medals read *Rhys Bailey Medals of Valor.* Harriet pulled one of the medals from the box to examine it more closely.

"Rhys earned a Victoria Cross?" she whispered. She recognized the style of the medal, an ornate cross on a burgundy ribbon, one of the highest awards a British soldier could receive. It would make sense for a middle-aged Rhys to have served in World War II, but she never would have guessed that he was a war hero. To earn the Victoria Cross, he must have done something incredibly brave and important in the enemy's presence. Surely a war hero of this caliber wouldn't have been involved in a nefarious way in the S&W Railway crash—would he?

On Tuesday morning, Harriet got things squared away at the clinic and let Polly know where she was headed. Then she, Ashley, and Trevor climbed into the Land Rover and headed in the direction of Finn O'Malley's.

Finn's farm was remote and just north of the track. As they drove farther out of town, residences dwindled from a few scattered homes to virtually none. Finn had mentioned that he enjoyed having plenty of space and privacy and that he didn't want to have to worry about any of the emus from his mob bothering other livestock.

A long lane led to Finn's home. When they arrived, Harriet parked the car and started to get out. Almost immediately, a man she assumed to be Finn burst out of the house, waving his arms wildly. "Get back in your car!"

Perplexed, Harriet looked around to see if she could find a reason for the man's panic. They were in the middle of nowhere. Surely there was no danger out here.

Then she saw the source of Finn's distress. An emu, its feathers ruffled up in a display of dominance, was barreling toward the Land Rover.

Harriet quickly got back in the vehicle and shut her door. She hadn't worked with emus much before and had been amused when Finn mentioned their aggressiveness. But after seeing one in person, she wasn't laughing.

Finn ran back to the porch. When he returned, he held something above his head.

Trevor laughed. "What's he doing with those feather dusters?"

Harriet watched as Finn waved the dusters and stared down the emu. "I think he's asserting dominance." A giggle rose in her throat as she watched the spectacle unfold through the windshield.

There was a complicated dance between man and bird, but Finn never broke his intense stare. After a few minutes, the emu stood down and Finn was able to fasten a rope around its neck and lead it to a fenced-in area a short distance from the house.

Finn tucked the handles of the feather dusters into the back pockets of his jeans. "Sorry about that," he said jovially as he approached Harriet's car. "I didn't know what I was getting into when I became an emu farmer. Reggs Harrison is temperamental, and I've had to learn on the fly, as it were."

Harriet slowly opened her car door. "The bird's name is Reggs Harrison? Like Rex Harrison, the actor?"

Finn laughed. "My wife is a huge Audrey Hepburn fan, and she loves *My Fair Lady*. She's not, however, a fan of Rex's character in the movie, so she combined his name with the word *eggs* to name our difficult emu. He doesn't play well with others. I'm sure he'll calm down when you work with him though."

Harriet was glad to hear that. She had to treat the entire mob for parasites today, and cranky Reggs Harrison would be included among them. She took a deep breath and tried to sound more confident than she felt. "I'm up to the challenge."

"If you're anything like Old Doc Bailey, I'm sure you are."

The mention of her grandfather reminded Harriet of his great-uncle Rhys. She knew she came from a good lineage with Grandad Harold, but what would it mean to find other family members were on the wrong side of history?

Finn ushered her group inside the farmhouse and settled Ashley and Trevor in the kitchen, where Finn's wife, Anna, plied them with cookies—or rather, biscuits—and tea.

A quick walk through the house showed plenty of family photos on the mantel and walls. Finn, a conversational sort, was delighted to share stories with Harriet.

"So your family has a long history in White Church Bay." Harriet peered at a framed black-and-white photo of some of Finn's ancestors.

"Yes, my mother's side has lived here for the past four generations." Finn picked up another frame and showed it to Harriet. "This is my mother's grandmother, who led quite an entertaining life. She had an artists' enclave at her home in London. She regularly hosted painters, musicians, writers—you name it. I'm sure she could have told some stories."

That caught Harriet's attention. Maybe Finn would know something about Adelaide Evergreen visiting White Church Bay. She had found some information, but nowhere near enough to paint a complete picture. More resources couldn't hurt.

"I'm sure it would've been fascinating to be a fly on the wall in her home. I don't suppose you know if she ever met an author named Adelaide Evergreen?"

"I couldn't say off the top of my head, but we may be able to find the answer. My wife found some journals and letters of my great-grandmother's that chronicle much of her adult life. She even compiled and self-published a volume of them."

"Really? How interesting. Where could I get a copy?"

"Let me check with Anna. I'm sure she would be happy to gift a copy to you."

He disappeared down a hallway and soon returned with a slim volume in his hands. He handed it to her, and Harriet flipped the book open to its index. A quick scan for *Evergreen* showed several references.

"Thank you, Finn. This could be helpful." She stuck the book in her satchel, eager to go through it as soon as she could. Outside, the low-throated drumming of emus reminded her of the reason she had visited the O'Malley farm.

"That's our cue." Finn put the picture back on the mantel. Then he showed Harriet outside to the fenced area where the emus were kept.

A quick survey revealed plenty of plucked feathers and unhappy animals. The mob was dealing with a common parasite that, fortunately, was easily treatable. Harriet returned to her car to retrieve the supplies she needed then said a silent prayer that Reggs wouldn't give her trouble. To her great relief, he was calm and easy to handle during his treatment.

"Glad Reggs has decided to behave for once," Finn called. "The others should be good as gold."

Harriet exited through the gate to get a hair tie from her satchel, which rested in the grass outside the fence. She'd worked up a sweat treating the mob and desperately needed to pull her hair away from her face.

She fished a scrunchie from her bag and smoothed her hair into a ponytail, glad she only had a few more birds to treat. She still needed to visit the Cinder Track and then finish up at the clinic. It wouldn't do to run out of energy before she'd gotten halfway through the day's work.

She finished treating the rest of the mob with no issues then searched the area for Reggs once more.

He was nowhere to be found.

She scanned the group of birds again, wondering if she'd missed him.

"Reggs Birdbrain Harrison!" Finn bellowed suddenly.

Harriet followed the sound of his voice. Reggs was outside the gate, stabbing his beak furiously at something on the ground.

"Daffy old bird!" Finn growled as he charged toward Reggs. "We should start calling him Houdini."

Reggs must have gotten out through the gate when Harriet fetched her hair tie. It hadn't even registered that the gate was unlatched when she'd come back.

Finn engaged in a staring contest with the bird again. No feather dusters needed this time. The intensity of Finn's stare was enough to deter Reggs.

The emu dropped whatever was in his beak and obediently stretched out his neck to allow Finn to leash him.

"What have you been up to this time, Houdini?" Finn scolded.

Harriet looked down at the source of the bird's fascination. The item that had lured him through the gate was none other than her satchel. In her haste to finish treating the mob, she hadn't closed the top.

She leaned in to expect the damage. Then she gasped.

Reggs had completely destroyed the book Finn had given her.

CHAPTER SEVENTEEN

Harriet's heart fell. She'd hoped the book would provide a window into the author's life and maybe also lend some insight on the crash. Now that hope was dashed. Not to mention the fact that the book Finn and Anna had so graciously given her was damaged beyond repair.

"Oh, no. I'm so sorry, Finn," she said. "I could've sworn I latched the gate."

Finn sighed and took the book from her, pinching what was left of the shredded pages between his fingers. "It's okay. Not your fault, at any rate. It's this bird. He's the one who busted loose. I should have been manning the gate."

"I hate to ask, but I'm desperate for any information on Adelaide Evergreen. I don't suppose there's anywhere I can purchase another copy of Anna's book, is there?"

Finn shook his head. "She printed a limited number of copies, and there aren't any more. Our personal copy is on loan to a family member who lives out of town."

There was nothing to be done then. Harriet finished her business with Finn and thanked his wife for her hospitality as they filed back through the house and out the front door.

Finn and Anna waved from the porch as Harriet, Ashley, and Trevor got into the Beast. As they pulled out of the drive, Ashley chuckled.

"What's so funny?" Harriet asked.

"Finn's wife must really love Audrey Hepburn. I heard him call one of the emus 'Eliza' and another one 'Doolittle.'"

A black SUV drove past right before Harriet pulled off the O'Malleys' lane and onto the main road. The smile died on her lips when she recognized the driver.

Ashley squinted through the windshield. "What's wrong?"

Harriet nodded toward the vehicle bouncing along on the road ahead of them. "That's Judith Martin."

"Who?" Ashley asked.

Harriet realized she hadn't caught Ashley up on all the details of the strange situation with Judith at the clinic. She quickly filled her in as she kept a close watch on the SUV.

"She seemed very concerned about the manuscript. After she left, I went into my office, and it looked like someone had gone through the papers on my desk."

Ashley raised an eyebrow. Then she glanced over her shoulder to peer through the back windshield. "Adelaide Evergreen's manuscript certainly has brought people out of the woodwork. Everybody and their brother wants to get their hands on it."

Harriet tightened her grip on the steering wheel. "The crash is a part of White Church Bay history. It affects the way people feel about the town and its residents. Even though it happened a long time ago, I think people still feel invested."

Harriet stayed close behind Judith's SUV. She still hadn't gotten ahold of the woman since the incident, and she needed to talk to her. Had Judith been snooping at the clinic that day? Why was she interested in the manuscript? Did she have a relative connected to the crash as well?

Harriet understood the desire to discover the truth, as well as the complex emotions that the search raised. The idea that her own relative may have been involved in the crash as a hero was intriguing. The possibility that he might have had a hand in causing it, less so.

The truth lay beneath the surface, regardless of what anyone thought. But would digging it up prove to be helpful or harmful?

Judith's SUV suddenly sped up, widening the gap between their vehicles until Harriet worried they might lose sight of her.

"What do we do?" Ashley asked.

"I say we floor it," Trevor piped up. "That's what people do in the movies when they're trying to keep an eye on someone."

Though the suggestion was appealing, Harriet did need to drive safely. She had a child in the car, after all, and the roads were particularly twisty and narrow.

Thankfully, she didn't have to worry about it because Judith slowed as they approached town and pulled into the car park they were headed for. Harriet parked a short distance away and sat in her car until Judith exited her vehicle and started for the Cinder Track. How strange that she'd led them to the very location they'd planned to visit.

"She has her dog with her," Ashley whispered to Harriet. "Are you sure he's friendly?"

Harriet considered it. Magnus had certainly seemed like a big sweetheart the day she'd assessed him at the clinic, but she knew that animals reacted differently in different contexts. German shepherds were large dogs and had the potential to be territorial.

"I think we're less likely to have any issues with him if we split up," she told Ashley and Trevor, digging the date nails out of her bag. "Plus, it'll save time if you guys go check these against the artifacts in the museum while I talk to Judith. Or try to."

"Are you sure?" Ashley asked.

"As sure as I can be," Harriet said. "I should be able to handle anything that happens, anyway."

Her misgivings clear on her face, Ashley led Trevor toward the museum.

Harriet went to intercept Judith. Best to be upfront about things and not beat around the bush. She needed to know if Judith had any information about the crash that Harriet didn't.

As Harriet drew closer to the woman, however, Magnus began growling.

Harriet bent down and extended her hand. "Hey, boy. Remember me?"

But Magnus remained on the defensive. His hackles were up, and his lips pulled back from his teeth in a snarl. Harriet noticed he wasn't on a leash.

"Don't worry. Magnus is impeccably trained. He's probably reacting to the smell of animals from the clinic." Judith didn't seem concerned at all and, oddly, she also didn't seem surprised to see Harriet. Had Judith somehow expected Harriet to follow her? It was suspicious that Judith's SUV had passed by Finn's farm—an otherwise remote area—at the same time Harriet had finished her call.

Harriet took the opportunity to pivot the conversation. The sooner she took care of matters, the better. "Speaking of the clinic—"

Judith beat her to the punch. "You'd like to know why I was snooping around."

"Well, yes." Harriet was taken aback. She'd expected Judith to be evasive, as she had been the day she'd visited the clinic.

Judith sighed. "I was looking for the manuscript. I read that piece in the *Whitby Gazette* about the discovery being made at your estate, and I had to know more."

"Why not ask me about it instead of invading my privacy?" Harriet asked. "I would've told you everything I knew."

"I didn't think you would, if you were anything like that Müeller woman at the museum."

"Petra?" Harriet asked.

Judith scowled. "Yes, Petra. She told me in no uncertain terms to get lost when I asked her about the manuscript. When I wouldn't back down, she threatened to call the detective constable on me for harassing her. When he showed up at your clinic, I thought she'd followed through on her threat."

Perhaps Judith was telling the truth. Her words matched up with Harriet's own experiences of the museum owner. Petra had seemed quite reluctant to relinquish control of the manuscript. And Judith had also seemed antsy at the clinic when Van arrived.

"How did you get into my house?" Harriet asked. "The door leading to the study is kept locked."

"It wasn't locked when I found it. Your desk gal, the one with the fuchsia streak in her hair, must've forgotten to shut it after she returned the manuscript."

Harriet gaped at her. "You're telling me that Polly left the door to my study open?"

Judith nodded. "To be fair, I think it was an accident. She was all aflutter as soon as that DC arrived."

"I suppose Polly let the dogs out of their crates too?"

"No. That was me." Judith ducked her head sheepishly. "I didn't want the animals or anyone else to get hurt. I only let one dog out to distract you so I could sneak a peek at the manuscript. The other dog must have busted the latch on his crate. By the time all the commotion was over, I realized you didn't have the information I needed anyway, so it was a wasted effort."

"What information did you need?"

"My great-aunt, Alice Wright, was involved in the S&W Railway crash. In fact, she died shortly after it happened. I want to learn more about her, but I haven't been able to. And your document was missing the chapter that supposedly talks about her in detail."

Alice Wright, who had corresponded with Rhys Bailey. "Actually, I may be able to help you. I think Alice and a relative of mine were a couple at one time."

Judith's voice gained a flinty edge. "I'm well aware of that. It's another reason I haven't asked information from you directly. I doubt you'd give me the truth. You wouldn't want to make your family look bad. But Rhys wasn't exactly perfect. He toyed with Alice's emotions then abandoned her when she needed him most."

Harriet had no idea how to reply. Rhys and Alice had cared deeply for each other. That was evident from Alice's side of their correspondence. It didn't make sense that he would have hurt Alice.

Yet there was the chapter that Robert had given her that implicated Rhys in the crash. What if Rhys had contacted Adelaide Evergreen—not to uncover the truth, but to bury his own guilt?

Harriet tried not to let her doubts show. "I can't believe Rhys would do that."

"I'm not daft, so don't treat me like I am." All pretense of friendliness had left Judith's demeanor, which now more closely matched Magnus's. The dog was no longer growling, but he was still on edge, watching Harriet with a hard gaze. "I've spoken with Robert Callum since I brought Magnus to the clinic. I know he gave you the missing chapter. That's all I want to see."

"I don't know the truth any more than you do," Harriet began, but Judith cut her off.

"Nonsense. You don't want to see your relative implicated. You're not interested in the truth."

Magnus let out a warning bark.

Harriet glanced over her shoulder to see Ashley and Trevor approaching. She motioned toward Magnus. "You might want to put your dog on a leash."

"He's very well-trained—" Judith started to say, but Magnus suddenly lunged away from her.

Ashley shrieked and shielded Trevor, but the dog wasn't interested in them. Instead, he ran past them and crashed into the woods.

"Ah, see? He was upset at an animal over there." Judith took a few steps in the direction Magnus had bolted and commanded, "Magnus, heel!"

The dog promptly burst from the surrounding trees and planted himself at Judith's side.

She clipped a leash on him before straightening to fix her gaze on Harriet. "I'd like to see the manuscript for myself."

Harriet returned her stare. "You'll have to take that up with the museum. They have the original."

"I've already tried that. I'd like to see your copy of the document."

"I'm not comfortable with that." Harriet didn't intend to back down. If someone out there was trying to erase Adelaide Evergreen's exposé from existence, her copy was at risk as well, and she certainly didn't trust Judith with it.

"Why do you care? I'm simply trying to vet it." Frustration roughened Judith's voice. "I need to make sure it doesn't paint your family in a positive light and my great-aunt in a poor one. I want to know what happened."

"So much that you're willing to break the law for it? You trespassed on my private property." The words came out a little sharper than Harriet had intended, and Judith's expression hardened into chiseled stone.

"I don't know what kind of cat-and-mouse game you're playing, Dr. Bailey, but I promise you one thing. The truth is going to come out about your family. Everyone's going to know what kind of person Rhys Bailey really was." She whirled on her heel and marched to her vehicle, Magnus sticking to her side like glue.

Harriet took a deep breath to calm herself as she watched Judith tear out of the lot. Then she turned to Ashley and Trevor. "I sure hope you made better progress than I did."

Ashley grimaced. "We couldn't get into the station. It's not open today. So we did some exploring and found a little rundown cabin about a hundred yards from the museum. The door was unlocked, so we went in. But we didn't stay. There was an old desk and a bed, and a suitcase was open on the floor."

Harriet sagged in disappointment.

"Don't get discouraged," Ashley said. "Not all is lost."

"Oh?"

"Trev and I are quite tenacious. When the museum didn't pan out, we walked along a section of track to see if our nails matched what was there. At first, I thought it would be useless to compare them, since the nails that are in the track now must have been replaced more recently than 1917. But then Trev realized there was a stamp symbol."

"What's that?" Harriet asked.

Trevor showed her one of the date nails they'd found at the cottage. "See the number for the year? '16' for 1916?"

"Yes."

"See the shape next to the number?"

Harriet squinted. She had overlooked it before, but there was a wobbly shape pressed next to the number.

"That's the stamp symbol," Trevor explained. "It means that the nail belonged to the S&W Railway line. The date nails in the Cinder Track now are from 1964, but they have the same stamp symbol."

So the nails among her family's heirlooms had belonged to the S&W Railway. They had tangible proof now. That was something, though what it meant for Rhys, Harriet had no idea. "Great work, Trevor," she said. "We'd be lost without you."

Trevor puffed out his chest. "I'm happy to help. Mom, is it okay if I go see if I can figure out what the dog was after in the woods?"

"As long as you're careful. Watch out for wild animals and poison ivy."

"I will." Trevor trotted onto the path that Magnus had taken when he'd bounded away.

"I thought that dog was going to eat us alive," Ashley told Harriet. "I wonder what he was chasing. A rabbit?"

"I don't know."

Trevor raced back to them, a glinting object in his hands. "I think it was a person. And I think they left this behind."

Trevor extended the item toward them. It was a lighter, and it appeared to be an antique.

"Where did you find this?" Harriet asked.

"It was right where Magnus ran. I could tell because the leaves were disturbed there."

Ashley leaned over to study the lighter. "Can you show us?"

"Sure." Trevor led them a short distance away to a clear patch before the trees. The area butted right up to the decommissioned station.

Whoever ran into the woods might have overheard Harriet's conversation with Judith.

CHAPTER EIGHTEEN

"Do you really think there was someone else at the track this afternoon?" Ashley asked as they walked into Harriet's house.

Harriet ran her fingers over the filigreed edge of the lighter. "I think so. Maybe someone was watching us."

"Why do you say that?" Trevor asked.

"If the lighter had been out in the elements for a while, it would show. But it's in pristine condition." Harriet set the lighter on the coffee table so everyone could see it. "Someone dropped it recently."

Ashley picked up the lighter to study it as Harriet had done. "Maybe Judith has an accomplice."

The thought made Harriet shiver. "It's possible. We need to find out who it belongs to."

"There are some words on here, but I can't tell what it says," Ashley said.

Harriet leaned over and squinted. Ashley was right. Hidden among the filigreed flourishes were words in another language. "Good catch, but I don't speak German. It starts, *Wer zwei Hasen*... What does that mean?"

"Beats me. I took French in school." Ashley looked thoughtful. "*Hasen* sounds familiar, though. Like Hasenpfeffer, which is rabbit stew. My grandmother was Dutch, and she used to make that dish. But I have no idea what the rest means."

"Good thing we can look it up!" Trevor said with a comical waggle of his eyebrows. "That's what Mom always tells me to do when I don't know the answer to something."

Ashley tousled his hair. "Yes, and look at you now. My very own walking encyclopedia."

Trevor seemed embarrassed but also pleased. "Mom you're messing up my hair."

"Spoken like a true preteen." Ashley laughed. "It's getting late, kid. Why don't you head on up to bed?"

"Aw, now? Things are just getting good."

Ashley blew out a mock sigh. "All right. Five more minutes."

Following Trevor's good advice, Harriet grabbed her laptop and typed the phrase engraved on the lighter into a translator site. *Wer zwei Hasen auf einmal jagt, bekommt keinen.*

"The phrase translates to 'He who chases two rabbits at once will catch none.'" Harriet blew a wayward lock of hair from her face. "Boy, isn't that applicable? I feel like I'm chasing rabbit trails with everything lately. Work, relationships, romance."

Trevor's eyes widened. "Romance? Yuck. Never mind. I'll head to bed now."

Harriet was sure his attitude would change in a few years, but for now, he retreated with a book tucked under his arm, leaving Ashley and Harriet in the sitting room.

"Romance, is it?" Ashley's eyes sparkled, and she pulled her feet up onto the couch. "Girl talk. This is what I came to England for."

Harriet laughed. "That's a long way to travel for girl talk."

"You're trying to distract me from the topic at hand, and it won't work. Are we talking about the hunky stranger at church who was making eyes at you?"

Harriet's cheeks warmed. "No, not Pascal." She brushed off Ashley's teasing and explained the connection between Pascal and her uncle Dom. She also filled Ashley in on the details of how Pascal was helping with the Adelaide Evergreen manuscript.

"Wow. Perfect timing."

"I know. It's like he showed up right when I needed him."

"Does he live in White Church Bay?"

"No. He lives in France."

Ashley raised her eyebrows. "That's a whole different country. Don't you think that's a little far away? Long-distance relationships can be tough."

Harriet snorted. "Ash, you're getting way ahead of yourself. I'm not interested in Pascal. We've barely met. Our relationship is strictly business."

But what was her plan if Will decided he wanted nothing more than friendship with her after all? Would she putter around her house and her clinic, alone for the rest of her life? Maybe Ashley was right. Maybe she should consider branching out. Even if she did care for Will, it felt good to have someone show such open interest in her as Pascal had. What little she knew of the man showed him to be charming and impressive.

Ashley frowned. "What about the pastor? Do you have feelings for him?"

Will's face floated into Harriet's mind, and butterflies took flight in her stomach. "I do. And I thought he felt the same way, but now I'm not sure."

Ashley raised her eyebrows. "You'd know if you saw how he looked at you on Sunday."

Ashley's words sparked a flicker of hope in Harriet, but she immediately smothered it. Talk about putting the cart before the horse. She didn't need to deal in wishful thinking. She wanted to stick to the facts. Unless Will asked her on a date, she would have to assume they were friends. She wouldn't hold him to words hastily spoken after a near-death experience, especially when there had been no follow-up.

She didn't say any of that to Ashley though. Her friend's hesitance to share emotions made Harriet reluctant to share as well. Instead, she cleared her throat and suggested, "Maybe we should get back to business."

Ashley reluctantly agreed. They hunkered down as the evening wore on, finally dating the lighter to the early twentieth century. They also discovered something else.

Ashley pointed to the flat bottom of the lighter. "I think I see initials here."

Harriet tried to decipher the letters. "*H…C*?"

"No. I think it's *H.G.*" Ashley tapped her fingers on the arm of the sofa.

An idea came to Harriet. "Wait a minute." She fetched Alice's letters and carefully searched through them until she found what she wanted. "Listen to this. It's from a letter dated winter of 1917. Alice writes, 'The man is new to the factory, but he knows enough to keep his lighter away from the guards. He must've hidden it somewhere outside and then collected it after work. It fell from his coat pocket as he was leaving, and I picked it up. As one of the only male line workers in the factory, he keeps to himself. I asked around for his name and got the answer Henry Barnett.'"

"But that's *H.B.*" Ashley tipped her head to the side.

"No, stick with me. There's a connection. Henry Barnett was actually a man named Hans Goebel. Ellie told me the night she called from the museum. And the lighter belonged to Hans. Possibly this lighter." Harriet carefully smoothed out the letter. "Listen to the rest of what Alice said. 'An air of suspicion hangs about Henry, and the girls all think he's aligned with the kaiser. Louise said that she spoke to him and detected a German accent. I'd dismiss it as paranoia except for the fact that I saw the lighter he dropped and the phrase on it was clearly written in German.'"

"This must be the same lighter." Ashley shook her head in disbelief. "But why would it show up at the station now?"

"I don't know," Harriet said. "But it's possible that we're on the right track with the family connection. Perhaps the Millers and Hans Goebel cooperated in the crash. The lighter might have been dropped by someone descended from one of those families. The easiest conclusion to draw is that the Müellers are behind all of this."

"We need to know what Rhys wrote back to Alice," Ashley said decisively. "If all the other information on the crash is being suppressed, perhaps that's an avenue they haven't cut off yet."

"And I have a guess as to who might have those letters. Judith Martin. But I think the chances of her willingly handing them over to us are slim to none. Especially after our encounter this afternoon."

Ashley raised her eyebrows. "She technically trespassed in your home. Couldn't you call the police over that? I would think that would be leverage."

"I don't know. It's been several days. I probably should've reported it at the time if I wanted the police to take it seriously. And she didn't take anything."

"Okay, we'll put that on the back burner for right now. We can wait until things cool off before we approach her again. But we'd better not wait too long. Petra and Judith seem at odds now, but what if the Müellers get to her? Or at the very least, get to her letters?"

Before Harriet could reply, the phone rang. She hurried to answer it. Hopefully it wasn't the mysterious silent caller again.

But no such shroud of mystery hung around the person who had dialed Harriet this time. As soon as she answered the phone, a strident voice met her ears. "What did you do with it? I know you stole it!"

Harriet recognized the voice at once.

Petra. And she did not sound pleased.

"What did you do with the manuscript?" The normally stoic woman's voice bordered on hysterical.

Harriet was confused. Petra must know Harriet didn't have the document. What was she thinking?

Before Harriet could gain her bearings, Petra charged ahead. "How did you even get into the museum? Was someone helping you? You know I can press charges over this. Trespassing *and* theft!"

"Wait, slow down." Harriet tried to keep her voice calm. "I don't know what you're talking about. I haven't been to the museum."

"Then how do you explain the manuscript's disappearance? From under my very nose, no less!"

Petra's words slowly sank in. "Wait a minute. Do you mean the original manuscript? The one we found in Aunt Jinny's cottage?"

"Of course!" Petra snapped.

Harriet took a deep breath to gather her composure. "I'm afraid you have the wrong person. I didn't take the manuscript. I have the copy you gave me, but that's all. And I've been in contact with someone in the legal profession who seems to think your taking possession of the original manuscript might not have been aboveboard." It couldn't hurt to mention the information Pascal had given her. If the manuscript grab had been unethical, maybe a reminder of potential legal recourse would shake some sense into Petra.

"Yes, I know you've been in contact with that snooping lawyer. And with Eleanor Caldwell too," Petra sneered. "Watch your back. That's all I can tell you."

She hung up.

Harriet stared at the phone in disbelief. After calling Van to alert him of the situation, she immediately punched in a new number.

Pascal answered on the first ring. "Harriet, how lovely to hear from you. To what do I owe the pleasure of this call?"

Harriet quickly summarized her conversation with Petra. "Someone stole the manuscript, and they think it's me. Do I need to seek legal protection?"

"You didn't take it, did you?"

"Of course not."

"Then you have nothing to worry about. They have no tangible proof you did anything wrong. Petra is trying to frighten you because she's frightened herself." His voice was soothing, and Harriet tried to believe him.

Whether she felt better or not, that didn't answer the question at hand. Who had taken the manuscript from the museum?

"Listen," Pascal said. "I can tell that you're upset. Why don't we meet tomorrow to discuss the matter further? I found out some information when I visited the museum today that I think you'll find interesting."

She would welcome the prospect to use Pascal as a sounding board. "Sure, we could meet tomorrow. I finish up at the clinic around four."

"That won't work for me. I have an errand to run then. Any chance you could step out early?"

Her schedule was free of appointments after two. If she didn't receive any emergency calls, it should be all right to meet Pascal around midafternoon. "I could do two thirty. Where would you like to meet?"

"You're the local. Do you have any favorite restaurants?"

Harriet wasn't certain she viewed herself as a local yet. She hadn't even lived in White Church Bay for a year, but she did know some wonderful places to eat. "I'm not sure if it's fancy enough for you, but Cliffside Chippy has delicious fish and chips."

"It sounds perfect. See you at half past two."

Harriet finished the call and hung up. With all the enemies she'd made lately, she felt hopeful to have the lawyer as an ally.

CHAPTER NINETEEN

Still rocked by the disappearance of the manuscript from the museum—which had managed to make the local evening news—Harriet arrived at work on Wednesday morning, puzzling over her next step.

As it turned out, Polly was on a mission of her own. "So, tell me again. What *exactly* did Van say when he called you Sunday evening?"

Harriet had already filled Polly in on the details of her conversation with the detective constable, but she relayed the information again. "Not much. He asked if you were upset with him. I said no. Then he asked why you were avoiding him, and I said you'd gotten the impression he was unhappy. I told him he needed to be open with you about his feelings, and he said he would."

"That's all? You're sure he didn't say anything else?"

"I'm sure. Why?"

Polly pulled her hair into a ponytail. "Nothing has changed. It's been days since you talked to him, and he hasn't breathed a word about why he's been so distracted lately. He did ask me to the Moonlit Seaside Walk this weekend though. That's a good sign, isn't it?"

Harriet pictured the scene. The walk was an annual event in White Church Bay. It took place at night, and from what she had heard, it was a magical experience to walk along the shore against a starry expanse.

Before she could stop it, she pictured herself strolling along the beach with Will. Just as quickly, she forced thoughts of him away. After their last interaction at church, she was fairly certain he viewed Chelsea in a more romantic light than he did her.

Harriet answered Polly's question. "I think Van asking you to the walk is a very good sign. Don't worry, Polly. I'm sure everything is fine. You're both probably making a mountain out of a molehill."

The phone rang, and Polly scooped up the receiver. After a short conversation, she scribbled some information on a piece of paper and handed it to Harriet.

"What's this?"

"Your next emergency call. It's Will at the rectory."

Harriet hadn't spoken to Will since Monday when she asked his advice about the mystery. She was happy to talk to him, but she wished it were under more pleasant circumstances than a vet call. Her enthusiasm was also hampered by the memory of Chelsea flirting with him at church. "What's the emergency?"

"Large dog with suspected broken hip. Will says he's worried transport will make the dog worse."

Will didn't own a dog, but maybe he was helping someone. She quickly loaded up the necessary materials, got into the Beast, and drove to the rectory.

She hurried up the walkway and knocked on the front door.

Will answered, his normally calm demeanor marked by distress. "Thank goodness you're here. Bruiser is in my study."

Harriet followed him down the hall into his study, where she noticed the camel figurine she'd given him for Christmas displayed front and center on the desk. It was hand-carved olive wood and came from Israel. Did it mean anything that he kept it where he would see it every day?

A large tan dog with black markings on his ears and muzzle huddled under the desk. Shaking herself free of her musings, Harriet focused on her patient.

"What a gorgeous English mastiff." She set her bag on the floor and dropped to her knees. The dog's tail was tucked between his legs, and he moved away from her when she reached out her hand. His subdued whine let her know he was in pain. "Hi, buddy. It's going to be okay."

After some careful maneuvering, Harriet managed to ease under the desk and coax the dog out. With Will's help, she moved Bruiser out into the hall where she had more room. She inspected his hind leg and hip.

"I'm glad you called me," she told Will. The concern in his eyes was evident. "How did he get injured?"

"I'm not sure. I let him out in the backyard, and he started chasing a squirrel. He jumped over a retaining wall, and then he started limping. It was hardly any distance. You don't think he broke something, do you?"

Harriet gently felt the dog's hip, murmuring soothing words when he whined in protest. "He didn't sprain anything. He's dislocated his hip. Some large dogs, including mastiffs, are particularly susceptible to hip dysplasia, and that can cause dislocation, especially when they make sudden moves. It's quite common."

"Thank goodness." A breath whooshed from Will's lips.

Yet another thing to admire about him. He had a gentle heart and sensitive spirit about animals.

Harriet carefully eased Bruiser's hip back into place and administered painkillers then went over some recovery instructions with Will. "Who does Bruiser belong to?"

"Chelsea Ward. I've been watching him since Sunday. Do you know her?"

"I do." The image of the woman hovering near Will after last week's church service was burned into Harriet's brain. But upon further consideration, perhaps she had misinterpreted their conversation. Maybe they hadn't been getting together for a date at all. "Is that why she was asking to meet on Sunday? So she could drop off Bruiser?"

Will tilted his head. "How did you know we were meeting?"

"I overheard her saying something about it as I was leaving the church."

"I didn't realize you were listening." He seemed slightly flustered. "Yes, that's why she asked to meet. Chelsea has helped out so much at the church that I certainly don't mind volunteering some of my time."

"That's nice of you." Harriet hoped Will would reveal more about his relationship, or lack thereof, with Chelsea.

But all he said was, "I'm happy to help. Thank you for tending to Bruiser."

"Of course." Harriet patted the dog's head. "He should be back to normal now. Try to keep him from being overly active for a while. His hip is probably still a little sore, and you don't want to risk a reinjury. Call me if you have any more issues."

"Certainly. Uh, I did have something unrelated to Bruiser that I'd like to ask—"

The loud ring of Harriet's cell phone cut him off, and she glanced at the screen. It was Polly, who wouldn't interrupt her unless it was important. "It's work. I have to get this."

Will pressed his lips together. "Of course. I'll speak to you later."

Harriet distractedly told him goodbye and hurried out to her car. Then she returned Polly's call.

Polly picked up at once. "Harriet, you need to get back here immediately."

The panicky tone in her voice reminded Harriet of past conversations about Van. "Is Van there, Polly? Simply tell him how you feel. I know it's difficult, but—"

"No!" Polly sounded irritated. "This isn't about Van, though the weirdness between us is why I'm calling you instead of him. It's about some man running around outside. He's holding a pair of hedge clippers, and he's scaring off the clients. A few people have pulled in and left already. I tried to go out and talk to him, but he refuses to listen."

Hedge clippers? Could it be Petra's gardener brother, Garrison? If so, he and Petra were looking guiltier by the minute—she the brains and he the brawn. Apparently, he meant to extend the threats in his sister's phone call.

Harriet turned the key in the ignition. "I'll be right there."

She sped to the clinic and parked her car. Sure enough, the lot in front of the building was deserted except for a bearded man wielding hedge clippers.

Harriet had an idea. She exited the vehicle and walked right up to him. "Garrison, this routine is getting old. Why do you keep showing up on my property?" If he had anything to do with the trespassing incident at the dower cottage, his knee-jerk response might give him away.

Garrison's eyes narrowed. "What are you talking about? I've never been here before."

"You haven't?"

"No."

"Then why are you here now?"

"Called in by the county to do some tree work. Limbs are too close to the power lines. See?" To demonstrate his point, he walked a short distance from the entrance and used the clippers to lop a limb from one of the trees that skirted her property.

Harriet followed him. "The county has never sent anyone before. I've always taken care of things myself."

"First time for everything."

"Do you have authorization from the village I could see?"

"No."

Harriet frowned. "This area is private property. I need to keep it clear for clients. I'd prefer it if you'd come back with the proper paperwork, please."

"I'm on a tight schedule, and I'm doing my job. I'm not going to be bossed around by the likes of you."

"Excuse me? What do you mean by that?" Harriet demanded.

In a few strides, Garrison closed the distance between them. "All right, since you insist on talking, I do have an account to settle. I'll have you know that my little sister was very upset after she spoke with you yesterday."

He was rather intimidating up close. A regular Paul Bunyan, to paint it in American terms.

Harriet took a step back. "I can't help how Petra feels. I am sorry about the manuscript going missing though."

"Are you sorry because you took it?" Garrison's voice dripped with accusation.

"No."

This wasn't going well. What if Garrison read her hesitation as an indictment of guilt? Harriet tried to make her voice firmer. "Listen, I want to know the truth about the train crash as much as anyone else. But I don't intend to twist the story my way."

It was the first time she'd been entirely forthright with the man, and she had no idea what his response would be.

Initially he looked shocked. Then a sneer twisted his features. "Is that so? You seemed pretty invested in getting ahold of chapter eighteen. Even tried to sway one of our workers to sneak about."

He meant Ellie. "It's well within my rights to want to know what's in the missing chapter. The museum employees have been acting strange about it."

"Not at all. We just don't want an outsider poking her nose in where it doesn't belong." He leveled a pointed glare at her. "Seems to me we aren't guilty of anything you haven't also done. You were upset to learn your relative was responsible for the crash. Weren't you?"

"Of course. Because it's a lie. He didn't do anything wrong." Harriet delivered her answer with confidence, but inside, a small part of her was unsure. The pieces of the puzzle were mixed up enough that she couldn't be entirely certain of the truth. What really happened with the train crash? Had Rhys Bailey been involved in a negative way?

Garrison was right. If Harriet searched her heart, she was reluctant to find someone in her own family guilty. But anyone would feel that way, wouldn't they? That didn't mean she would resort to threatening people or doctoring documents to hide the truth, as it seemed the Müellers had done.

"You need to go," she told Garrison. "Come back when you get clearance from the village to be on my property and can show me the paperwork to prove it."

Garrison glared at her then snapped the blades of his clippers shut. "Fine. But bear this in mind. I know you've ignored previous warnings, but I'd advise you to stop poking around, Doc. It's not going to make you or your business look any better. Best take responsibility for the ill your family caused."

He left, with his words ringing in Harriet's ears.

An ache settled inside as she watched Garrison's truck peel out of the lot. She felt completely outnumbered. Everyone seemed convinced that Rhys was responsible for the crash. Even the items she'd found in her family's memorabilia pointed to a conclusion she was hesitant to explore.

Her reverie ended when she noticed smoke rising from a ditch outside the tree line. Garrison must have been burning the branches he had felled.

Harriet immediately went to fetch a bucket of water to douse the flames. The last thing she needed was a wayward spark starting a fire near her clinic and home.

She threw water on the fire before she realized what it was Garrison was trying to burn.

The half-burned books were barely recognizable, but she spotted a familiar sticker on one of the spines.

The entire library collection of books on the S&W Railway crash had been feeding the flames.

CHAPTER TWENTY

Garrison's sudden appearance, as well as what he had left behind, rattled Harriet. She fished the remains of the books from the ditch and made a note to call the library once she figured out what to say. She also called Van again, even though she was starting to feel like a broken record.

By midafternoon, her stomach growled loud enough that she couldn't ignore it. Thankfully, she could look forward to her late lunch with Pascal at the Cliffside Chippy. She hoped he would have some advice for her.

She parked her Land Rover at the car park then walked to the restaurant. It was chilly, but the sound of seabirds and surf mingled pleasantly to smooth over any discomfort caused by the cold walk. As she drew close to her destination, Harriet could smell the delicious scent of fish and chips. The cozy stone building pulled her in like a magnet as she burrowed deeper into her coat.

She entered the restaurant and closed the door on the brisk, damp wind outside. A glance around the small establishment showed Pascal sitting at a corner table. He was extremely handsome in loafers, slacks, and a blue sweater that brought out the striking color of his eyes. The flecks of gray at his temples lent him a distinguished air.

He waved her over. "Harriet, over here."

When she reached his table, he stood and gathered her hands in his in an enthusiastic greeting. She was close enough to notice he smelled pleasantly of cologne and fresh seaside air. When he dropped her hands, she noticed something white poking from his sleeve.

His gaze followed hers, and he chuckled. "I suppose I was in a rush this afternoon. Reminder to self—cut the price tag from a shirt *before* you put it on. And here I was trying to impress you."

Harriet raised her eyebrows. "Impress me? Why?"

"If you can't tell, then I must make an effort to be more obvious."

Harriet wasn't sure what to make of his flirtations. Maybe Ashley was right. Maybe Harriet should be open to getting to know Pascal better, manuscript aside. She knew how she felt about Will, but if he didn't share her feelings, why should she sit around pining?

They didn't have to wait long for a server to take their order. Winter was a slow tourist season, and the restaurant reflected that. Harriet ordered an iced tea, and Pascal ordered water and a black coffee.

Pascal took a sip of coffee and then got to business. "Let me see if I'm clear on what's happened so far. You found the manuscript, the museum gave you a copy with a missing chapter, and then they gave you what you hope is a fake chapter but they claim is the original. Is that right?"

"It is, though it sounds extra chaotic summed up that way. And now, to complicate matters further, the entire manuscript is missing from the museum."

"Any guesses who might have taken it?"

"I have a few ideas."

She filled him in on her recent interactions with the people involved—Ellie, Robert, and Judith, as well as Petra and Garrison—and told him of her suspicions that Judith was working with the Müellers to suppress the manuscript. Then she pulled the lighter that Trevor had found at the Cinder Track from her purse and set it on the table. "I think this belongs to one of the people I mentioned. I should've taken it to the authorities immediately. I practically have the detective constable on speed dial by now. But I got distracted by Petra's phone call."

He turned the lighter over in his hands and studied it thoughtfully. "I can't speak to Judith's involvement, but I do have something to say about Robert and the Müellers. They are definitely up to no good. I visited the museum early this week to tell them to release the document to me, but they refused."

"I can't say that surprises me," Harriet said.

Pascal shook his head. "I think they knew it would take time to get the necessary paperwork through the system. I told them they had no legal footing, but it was like talking to a brick wall."

That sounded familiar. "So you struck out completely?"

"Not quite." The corner of Pascal's mouth twitched. "I lingered outside the museum to contact my clients with the Evergreen estate. While I was waiting to hear back from them, I overheard Petra talking to Robert in the courtyard. The hedges were tall enough that they couldn't see me, but I could hear them. Petra reminded Robert that he was in their employ, not the other way around. She told him that he needed to stick to the original plan or he could kiss his job goodbye."

Harriet wondered if that was why Robert was so agitated when he showed up at her house demanding Pascal's number. She told Pascal about the encounter. "He seemed pretty upset that he couldn't get ahold of you. Have you been speaking to him about the manuscript?"

Pascal took a sip of coffee. "I'm not getting anywhere with the Müellers, so I've been corresponding mainly with Robert. He's been fielding questions from the estate, though I think all the legalese has made him jumpy."

"He was more than jumpy when he showed up at my house the other night. He was angry. He said he couldn't get through to your firm. He got a recording that said the number wasn't in service." Harriet hated that she felt even a shred of doubt about her uncle's colleague, but really, hadn't this whole situation over the manuscript taught her that no one was who they seemed?

Pascal waved off her concerns. "I told you. The number hadn't transferred yet. It has now. You can try it and see for yourself. Yvette should pick up."

Harriet dug her phone from her purse and dialed the number on the front of Pascal's card.

Sure enough, a woman answered amid a background of busy activity. "Paris Legal Alliance. This is Yvette Allard for Pascal King. How may I direct your call?"

Harriet glanced at Pascal. What now? She didn't have any business with the firm. He motioned for her to hand the phone to him, and he chatted easily with the receptionist, asking a few questions about cases that sounded like Latin to Harriet's ears. She relaxed as he finished the conversation and disconnected.

The server appeared again to take their food order. It was a welcome break from sleuthing. At Harriet's insistence, Pascal ordered fish and chips with a side of vinegar for his meal. When the waitress brought them plates piled high with golden fish and fries, Pascal's eyebrows rose with approval. He took a bite of fish.

"I've had this dish before and wasn't impressed," he said. "But this is delicious."

"That's because it's so fresh," Harriet explained. "If you want to kick it up a notch, try the vinegar."

"I must admit, I've never used vinegar as a dipping sauce." Pascal dipped a fry into the cup of vinegar before taking a bite. His eyes widened. "Amazing. I would have expected it to overwhelm the fry, but they actually complement each other."

"That was exactly what I thought the first time I tried it." Harriet laughed.

Before long, Pascal had cleared his plate. He set it aside and leaned back in his chair with a sigh of satisfaction. "So, let's talk business. We need to know if anyone else has information about the crash outside of the manuscript."

Harriet told him of her recent discovery that Judith's great-aunt had been acquainted with Rhys. "The two of them corresponded before the crash. The letters Alice wrote to Rhys tell part of the story, but not all of it. Judith might have the letters he wrote."

"We should try to get those letters. It could fill in the blank spaces of the mystery." Pascal focused his piercing blue eyes on Harriet. "It's important that you talk to Judith. I'll keep working on the Müellers and others at the museum."

Though Harriet was reluctant to approach Judith again, she agreed. After all, Pascal wasn't asking her to do anything he wouldn't. He was wading into the fray as well, and it made sense for her to speak to Judith, since they were already acquainted.

When the server brought the bill, Pascal smoothly slid it away from Harriet. "The meal is on me. I can write it off as a business expense. Though I must confess, it's been more pleasure than business."

Harriet felt her cheeks warm. Even if she wasn't interested in the man the way she was Will, he was certainly handsome and charming. Thankfully, Pascal didn't comment on her blushing. He had already taken the bill to the register to pay.

Pascal returned to the table. "Thanks for a delightful afternoon. Since you're so busy, I'd be happy to take the lighter by the police station for you." He motioned to the lighter that still sat on the table. "I'm killing time until I hear back from the Evergreen estate again."

"That would be helpful. Thank you."

"Wonderful. I'll keep you in the loop." He bid her goodbye, assuring her that everything would end well.

She hoped he was right.

White Church Bay
Winter 1917

Rhys hurried toward the railway station. He was later than he would've liked, but the cattle had broken through their fence, and he'd spent the better part of his afternoon and evening rounding them up.

Alice didn't know he was coming to meet her. In fact, she had expressly forbidden him. Her little brother, Jimmy, brought the message. That hint of the headstrong young girl she was when they first met still showed through. At least the war hadn't stripped her of all she had been before going to the factory.

He had to go to the station though. He had to meet her there. Her last few letters had grown increasingly worrisome. Not only had she engaged in conversation with Henry, she'd also followed him. Then she waited outside the lodging house until he left for dinner. With him gone, she said it was easy to break into his room. When she held Henry's letter to the still-glowing embers of the fireplace to read it, more words appeared with the heat.

A secret letter lay underneath the surface of a decoy.

Alice concluded that he'd written the words in invisible ink concocted from something that had been on his socks.

> I thought Henry was planning an explosion at the factory with as much as he flaunts that lighter of his. But his letter hints at something bigger. A train crash.

Alice gave Rhys all the details from the letter Henry wrote.

> He is planning something to cause the crash, and he doesn't seem to care if he lives or dies as a result. He told me he's dying, and his letter

confirmed that. He has a liver condition that will likely be fatal to him in the next year. His real name is Hans Goebel, and he is a native of Hamburg.

The man Alice had followed was dangerous. A criminal. She had already endangered herself by approaching him. He must be suspicious of her. But to break into his room and root through his belongings—well, it was a wonder she had escaped without Hans knowing.

Rhys still dreamed of a life beyond the borders of the war. A life where he and Alice could get married and raise a family on a plot of land. He daydreamed of taking walks along the coast while the children dug in the sand for treasures on the beach at low tide.

He wanted Alice safe more than anything. If he had to injure her feelings to keep her so, he would. He answered her letter with lies meant to protect her and discourage her from riding the train on the night she'd mentioned.

I think you're just being paranoid. Henry is no more a spy than a doddering eccentric. Ink from socks and invisible letters, indeed. Are you sure you aren't inventing stories? You know you haven't felt well since you began work at the factory. What if this is a figment of your imagination, drummed up after one of your headaches?

The farm is failing, and I need to focus on making money to save it. I can't continue to support these delusions of yours. You'd do well to hang them up too.

He hoped it hurt him more to write the accusing words than it did her to read them. But no. Her only reply was the message via Jimmy to stay away. Whether she was trying to protect him or her own feelings by her silence, he didn't know.

He arrived at the station ten minutes before the train was slated to arrive. He had little time to walk the track for any sign of the sabotage Alice had warned of.

It was dark, so he heard the train before he saw it. A low rumble from somewhere down the line mixed with the sound of nighttime surf. It was a familiar lullaby, no longer soothing because of what Alice had told him.

The train rounded the corner, its singular headlight bearing down on him. Then he watched in horror from the platform as the engine car hit an invisible snag. The long whistle of the operator was the only warning, and it was too little too late.

The train derailed as if in slow motion. First, the engine car then the passenger cars. Rhys stood rooted to the spot, unable to take his eyes from the horrific scene before him or to shut out the thunderous screeching and crashing of metal on metal. Only when the train had stilled was he able to move again, and he immediately sprinted toward the cars.

Where was Alice?

The thought reverberated in his brain, even as others ran around him calling loved ones' names. The train's headlight had come to rest at a strange angle, casting eerie shadows all around.

Rhys pushed forward, unable to give up until he saw Alice for himself.

When he found her, she was stumbling along the length of the train. She grabbed his arms and babbled something about losing Hans in the commotion. "I kept an eye on him the whole ride, Rhys. I thought he was going to take out the driver, but he must have done something else to cause the crash."

"That's not important now," Rhys assured her, holding her elbows to support her. "Are you all right? Are you hurt anywhere?"

"I think I'm okay, but I heard someone say there might be a chemical leak from one of the cargo cars."

His stomach, which had eased with her first words, tightened again. "Chemical?"

"Yes. The train was carrying phosgene to the front lines. It's a choking agent used for chemical warfare." She lapsed into a coughing fit that was particularly bothersome after what she'd just told him.

"Alice?"

She managed a few deep breaths. "I'm all right. Come on. We have to help the others."

Though Alice continued to cough, she didn't stop their search and rescue. Together, the two of them pulled seven people from the wreckage.

Then Alice fixated on Hans again. "I wonder if he ran into the woods. We'll never find him with how dark it is now.

Or what if he's stealing cargo? I saw some people going toward the woods, carrying things from the crash."

"Alice," Rhys began. He was concerned about her, and her obsession with Hans wasn't helping.

She went on as if he hadn't spoken. "What if those people were helping him flee to safety? Back to whoever hired him to do this? I know you don't believe me about Hans, and you think I'm being crazy, but I can't just let him fade into the mist. He can't get away with this, Rhys."

"I'm sorry," he told her. "I didn't mean what I said in my letter. I don't think you're crazy at all. I believe you. I was trying to keep you safe, hoping you'd stay away from Hans if I discouraged you."

"One thing you should know about me is that will only make me dig my heels in even more," she said.

"I'll keep that in mind next time I tell you not to do something."

She raised her eyebrows at him, but there was a hint of a smile at the corner of her mouth. "You think there'll be a next time?"

Emboldened, he wrapped his arms around her. "I'm counting on it."

The sense of dread Rhys had lived with for months finally began to ebb as he held Alice. The worst had happened. What more could they fear?

CHAPTER TWENTY-ONE

The week had been so eventful that Harriet nearly forgot about the ladies' tea that Aunt Jinny was hosting Wednesday evening. As soon as she finished up work at the clinic, she raced to the cottage.

"Thank goodness you're here," Aunt Jinny cried as Harriet burst through the door. "I could use a second set of hands about now. Where are Ashley and Trevor?"

Harriet shrugged out of her coat. "Trevor woke up with a cough this morning. He and Ashley have been taking short train trips from Whitby to nearby towns while I'm working, and you know how germs circulate through those enclosed cars. We think it's a cold. He's not running a fever, but Ashley is keeping him away just in case."

Ashley had told her that while Trevor rested she had plans to forge ahead with the mystery. Maybe she would figure out another piece of the puzzle by the time Harriet got home.

Aunt Jinny's forehead crinkled with concern. "I hope he's all right. Tell Ashley I'm happy to check on him if he starts feeling worse."

"I'm sure she would appreciate that." Harriet hung up her coat. "What can I help with?"

"How do you feel about kitchen duty?"

"I'm on it."

Aunt Jinny led Harriet to the kitchen. "The sweets are all ready to go." She pointed to a couple of platters piled impressively high with tarts and biscuits. Harriet's mouth watered at the sight, and she reluctantly ignored the tempting treats as Aunt Jinny gave her instructions.

"What I need your help with is the tea sandwiches. We're making—or rather, *you're* making—three types. Cucumber with cream cheese, roast beef with horseradish, and egg salad with watercress. All your supplies are here. Please don't forget to cut off the crusts."

Harriet surveyed the array of ingredients her aunt had set on the counter. She had her work cut out for her, but she was certain she could whip things into shape. "I've got it under control."

"Wonderful. Thanks for your help, love. I'm running late because I had an emergency appointment with a patient right before you arrived. I'm going to go finish tidying up." Aunt Jinny squeezed Harriet in a tight hug before hurrying away.

The time sped by as Harriet assembled the sandwiches. Before long, she had almost filled a three-tiered tray with them. She slid the last cucumber sandwich onto the top tier and stood back to admire her work just as Aunt Jinny entered the room to make tea. It wasn't long until there was a hearty knock at the door.

Aunt Jinny clapped her hands together. "The first arrival is here. You ready?"

Harriet blew out a breath and smoothed her hair from her face. "I think so. Open the floodgates." She was more excited for the event than she'd realized. Time off from thinking about Adelaide Evergreen's manuscript was just what the doctor ordered.

Aunt Jinny hurried to the door and opened it to admit Polly with a pie.

"You're the first one here." Aunt Jinny waved her through the door. "Come inside where it's warm."

As Aunt Jinny closed the door behind Polly, the cottage landline rang.

"Care to get that, Harriet?" Aunt Jinny asked. "I'll get Polly settled in."

"Sure." Harriet hurried to the phone and picked it up. "Dr. Garrett's residence. This is Harriet."

"Harriet?" It was Ashley on the other end of the line, and she sounded harried. "I'm so sorry to bother you, but some people are here, and they want to talk to you."

"Face-to-face," ordered a voice in the background that Harriet recognized at once. "Tell her we want to talk in person."

Petra Müeller.

Harriet excused herself, leaving Polly to help Aunt Jinny in her absence, and hurried home.

Ashley opened the front door. "Thank goodness you're here. There's a group of people who want to talk to you about the manuscript. They're waiting for you in the living room. I told them you were busy, but—"

"It's all right." Harriet braced herself before entering the living room, where she found that the group included not only Petra but also Robert Callum and Judith Martin.

Judith locked eyes with Harriet. "Just the person we want to talk to."

Harriet wasn't sure what the woman could have to say to her after their last conversation. She had assumed Judith was interested in the manuscript because of her relative, Alice Wright. Now, it was clear that Petra and Judith had made amends and Judith was familiar with the group at the museum. Who knew what the three of them might have discussed in the meantime? Whatever it was, they clearly stood united against Harriet.

Harriet tried her best to be polite, but to say she was getting frustrated with all of them was putting it mildly. "Now isn't a good time to meet. I'm supposed to be helping my aunt with an event. Can't this wait until tomorrow?"

"We'll make it quick," Petra retorted. "But we're not leaving until we hash things out."

"Judith came to the museum today," Robert said. "She told us about your conversation at the Cinder Track, and she showed us the letters your relative wrote to her great-aunt. It appears he was skeptical of her attempts to find the saboteur, and in one of them he wrote that he would stop her 'by any means possible.'"

Harriet didn't know what to say. It wasn't as if she knew what was in Rhys's letters. Yet how could she trust anything these three told her about their contents? They all had a secret motive, a hidden agenda. Even Ellie had been keeping secrets.

"Let's cut to the chase. What we really want to know is who took the manuscript from the museum." Judith's tone verged on demanding. "The only possibility we could agree on was you."

She was dumbfounded. "Me? Why would you think I took it?"

Trevor appeared at the foot of the stairs, and Ashley left the group to tend to him.

Petra picked up the conversation. "One, you were at the museum right before it went missing. The security camera footage proves that. It shows the papers on Robert's desk, and then you enter the room with your back to the camera and a large bag on your shoulder. By the time Robert enters, the papers are gone."

Harriet protested. "They fell on the floor. Surely the footage showed that."

"We're not finished," Judith said firmly. "Two, things aren't looking good for Rhys Bailey's involvement with the crash. You heard what was in one of the letters he wrote to my aunt. Naturally you'd want to protect his name."

"And three," Robert chimed in with a glare. "You told Eleanor that you regretted taking the manuscript to the museum in the first place. That if you could do it over, you wouldn't have made it public. Perhaps you decided to make it private once again."

Harriet blew out a breath. She had said that in confidence to Ellie. It was frustrating that Petra had used her status as an authority to talk Harriet out of ownership of the manuscript, especially since Pascal thought Harriet and Aunt Jinny might have some kind of legal claim to it along with the Evergreen family. "I didn't steal the manuscript. I'm trying to figure out the truth like everyone else."

"Are you?" Robert asked. "Seems to me you're more concerned with keeping your family's name squeaky clean."

"I hope that's what the truth reveals, but—"

"But nothing," Petra sneered. "You'll do anything to protect your family's reputation, including stealing a priceless artifact from the people who want to see it cared for and protected."

Before Harriet could think of a reply, Ashley hurried down the stairs with a thermometer clutched in her hand. "Trev's spiked a fever, Harriet. It's over a hundred and three. Should I take him to the hospital?"

Harriet tried to ease her friend's mind. "I'll call Aunt Jinny. She'll know what to do."

She left the group in the living room and used the landline to call her aunt.

"Bring him over," Aunt Jinny said. Lively chattering in the background told Harriet that more guests had arrived for the ladies' tea. "I can look at him in the clinic."

Harriet relayed the message to Ashley, who quickly bundled Trevor in his winter coat and hat. His cheeks were flushed, his eyes glassy. Ashley put an arm around him to steady him as they navigated to the front door. "Don't worry, buddy. We'll get you feeling better soon."

Harriet ushered Petra, Robert, and Judith out of her house in hopes that they would leave. Instead, Judith stayed close behind Harriet and pointed to a police vehicle parked in front of the house.

"Did you call the authorities about the video footage?" Judith asked Robert.

Robert shook his head. "Petra?"

"It wasn't me." Judging from Petra's wide eyes, Harriet guessed that, for once, she was telling the truth. Then the surprise on Petra's face was replaced with determination. "But you better believe I'll be asking him how I can obtain a warrant to search this property for that missing manuscript."

Surprisingly, however, the three accusers skirted Van's vehicle and left before he stood in the car park.

Harriet exchanged a concerned glance with Ashley as Van climbed out of the car. Then she hurried toward him.

"What are you doing here, Van?" His flashing lights weren't on, so it wasn't an emergency. Was it?

Her distress must have shown on her face, because Van rushed to reassure her. "No need for alarm. Just making the rounds again, since you had that trespasser here the other night and our cat burglar lead didn't pan out." He peered down at Trevor. "Is he all right? He looks a bit peaked."

"He's not feeling well," Harriet explained. "We're taking him to my aunt."

"Poor fellow. I won't hold you up." Van stepped out of the way to allow Ashley, Trevor, and Harriet to pass by him into the cottage.

Aunt Jinny's home had filled up quickly as more guests arrived, and the sitting room and kitchen were full of women balancing plates of food and cups of steaming tea. Harriet wove past them and followed Ashley and Trevor into Aunt Jinny's exam room.

Aunt Jinny began taking Trevor's vitals while Ashley stood close by.

Polly entered the room. "How's he doing?"

"Okay, but I'm sure he doesn't feel the best," Aunt Jinny replied. "The guests doing okay out there, Polly?"

"They're doing great. The refreshments are a hit."

"Thanks to Harriet." Aunt Jinny smiled at her as she wrapped a blood pressure cuff securely around Trevor's arm. As air filled the cuff, he started to protest about it being too tight, but Polly stepped in. She quickly engaged him in an animated conversation about trains, which seemed to distract him from his discomfort.

As Aunt Jinny was recording Trevor's blood pressure, a knock on the door sounded. "Come in."

Van poked his head around the door. "Everything looks good. No signs of any intruders or trespassers anywhere."

"Thank you so much, Van." Aunt Jinny smiled at him.

Van caught sight of Polly. "Are we still on for the Moonlit Seaside Walk this weekend?" he asked.

"Yes." Polly granted him a bright smile. "I'll see you then."

"Perfect." Van lit up at her enthusiasm.

Polly followed Van out to tell him goodbye, and Harriet peeked into the cottage to check her aunt's guests, who were still conversing and enjoying refreshments.

When Polly came back inside, Harriet raised her eyebrows at her friend. "See? Van is smitten with you. How could you doubt it?"

Polly laughed and bumped her shoulder against Harriet's. "Okay. You were right. Is that what you want to hear?"

Harriet smiled at her friend. "I'm just happy you're happy."

They reentered the exam room to see how Trevor was doing.

Aunt Jinny was in the process of relaying her diagnosis to Ashley. "The bad news is he has the flu. The good news is he's young and healthy and should be over it in no time. I'll write a prescription for an antiviral, and you can add over-the-counter medication. That should make him more comfortable. And remember, lots of fluids and rest."

Ashley looked relieved. "Thanks so much for checking on him."

"Of course."

Harriet ushered Ashley and Trevor to the door so they could head back to her house for the night. Quiet reined now that Petra, Robert, and Judith weren't there. Their appearance had added more stress to an already lively evening.

The ladies' tea continued without any further interruption, and Aunt Jinny led a wonderful devotional on the value of friendship. The next thing Harriet knew, it was time to help clean up. She munched thoughtfully on one of the remaining pistachio swirl biscuits as she bused plates and cups to the kitchen.

The truth of Trevor's flu diagnosis was a relief to Ashley, but neither Petra, Judith, nor Robert wanted to listen to the truth Harriet had to share, even when faced with it outright. Prior to this mystery with the manuscript, Harriet might have had a tough time sympathizing with that viewpoint. But now, she understood. Confronted with the possibility that a member of her own family might have been an unsavory character, all she wanted was to stick her head in the sand and ignore the evidence in front of her.

Could she be brave enough to face reality, even if the truth wasn't pretty?

CHAPTER TWENTY-TWO

Thursday morning at the clinic flew by in a maelstrom of appointments interspersed with a few texts to Ashley checking on Trevor. Thankfully, he seemed to be doing reasonably well and was powering through a stack of books, according to Ashley.

As lunchtime drew close, Harriet checked her schedule on the computer. "I'm going to take a quick break to run some errands," she told Polly. "I should be back before our first appointment this afternoon."

"No problem," Polly said.

On the way to her car, Harriet called Ashley. "Anything I can pick up for you or Trevor while I'm out?"

"I think we're all set," Ashley replied.

Trevor mumbled something in the background.

"Except for maybe some jelly beans? Trev has a craving."

Harriet made a mental note. Jelly beans weren't her first pick when she felt under the weather, but if they brought Trevor comfort, she was on board. "No problem."

She took the Beast into town, purchased some clinic supplies, and procured the promised sweets. She was on her way back to the clinic when her cell phone rang.

She answered the call with her hands-free system. "Hello?"

But as with the calls she'd received before, there was no answer.

"Hello? Who is this?"

This time, she thought she detected the faintest hint of breathing on the other end of the line.

"I can report this number for harassment, you know."

She barely got the words out when a dog barked in the background. The caller *did* have a dog, as Polly had mentioned the other day. And it sounded like a large dog too. Maybe a Doberman? Or perhaps a German shepherd?

"Judith Martin, I know that's you," she said. "Stop calling me."

The caller hung up.

"Got you," Harriet said with satisfaction. Hanging up was as much an admission of guilt as Harriet was likely to get from Judith. And now was as good a time as any to confront her about the letters she had from Rhys to Alice.

After a quick call to Ashley to let her know Trevor's candy would be delayed, Harriet struck out for Judith's house. She prayed Judith would be there. Harriet had the letters that Judith's great-aunt Alice had written to Rhys in her bag. Now she planned to use them as leverage if she needed to.

Within fifteen minutes, she pulled up in front of a modest but well-kept house. Harriet recognized the vehicle parked outside as the same one Judith drove the day Harriet had followed her to the Cinder Track. At least that was one hurdle cleared. Judith was home. But there was no guarantee that she would talk to Harriet.

Harriet got out of the Land Rover and walked toward Judith's porch. As she drew close to the front door, she could hear barking from inside. That must be Magnus. Hopefully, he would be in a better humor today than he was the last time she had seen him.

Harriet rapped on the front door and was surprised when Judith immediately answered. Magnus stood like a sentinel at her side. "What are you doing here? Decide to come clean about the manuscript?"

Harriet shook her head. "How many times do I have to tell you? I don't have it. I'm looking for it, the same as you." She fished Alice's letters out of her bag and held them up so Judith could see them. "Would I bring these otherwise? If I was so interested in clearing Rhys Bailey's name that I'd be willing to break the law, why would I admit these exist? Why wouldn't I destroy them?"

Judith narrowed her eyes. For a moment, Harriet thought she would order her away. Instead, Judith waved her inside. "Well, come on in, then. I don't want to settle things on the stoop. Let's hash it out like civilized human beings over a cuppa."

She led Harriet into the sitting room, Magnus right behind them. As Judith brought in a teapot and teacups, he settled on a rug in front of the hearth where he could keep an eye on the women.

"Milk or sugar?" Judith asked once she had poured steaming Earl Gray into two cups.

"A splash of milk, please."

Judith seemed pleased by Harriet's answer. "You almost sound like a good British citizen."

"I'm getting there." Harriet was surprised to feel a smile twitch at the corners of her lips.

"Now, then. Let's see these letters. You say my great-aunt wrote them?"

"Yes." Harriet spread the letters out on a clean space on the table. "See for yourself. Alice and Rhys seemed to care for each other a great deal. And for White Church Bay. They were trying to track a spy who worked at the same munitions factory Alice did."

"Henry Barnett?" Judith asked.

"Yes. Or Hans Goebel, as he apparently revealed in a secret letter he wrote to his superiors—a letter your great-aunt found. She wasn't able to prevent the train crash, but I believe she tried. I'd like to think Rhys did too, at least in the beginning. I don't know what happened between the two of them right before the crash though. They must've had a disagreement about something. Do you know?"

In answer, Judith rose and shuffled into another room. She returned with an antique hatbox from which she removed a stack of yellowed envelopes. She offered them to Harriet. "He didn't believe her. Simple as that."

Harriet gingerly opened one of the envelopes and read the faded words her great-great-granduncle had penned over a hundred years earlier. "'I think you're just being paranoid. Henry is no more a spy than a doddering eccentric… What if this is a figment of your imagination, drummed up after one of your headaches?'" She looked up from the letter to lock eyes with Judith. "Ouch."

"I can't imagine how a letter like that must have affected her," Judith said. "He basically told her that she should be committed to an asylum or something. Then he said he had to stop focusing on the saboteur because he needed to make money to save his family farm. He was at the station the night of the crash, as well as the day after. A witness from the railway saw him. I think the chapter Petra gave you is the real one. Rhys chose money over my great-aunt Alice. He engineered the crash and then stole the cargo to resell. His family—your family—benefited from his dishonesty."

"I can see how you'd get that theory from this letter," Harriet admitted. "But what if there's another explanation?"

Judith grunted and set her teacup in its saucer with a clatter. "He abandoned her, and now you're trying to protect him. I won't stand for it. Nothing could convince me you're not behind this mess in some form or fashion. It was a mistake to invite you in. I can't believe I tried to make amends."

They had so little information to paint a picture of the past. Letters, a few articles, and whatever information the manuscript offered—if it was even reliable. They had to read between the lines and figure out how to interpret reality.

Harriet had offered Judith everything at her disposal, but the woman still saw a different view of the crash than Harriet did. How to convince her that Rhys Bailey had been an upright person? Someone who was loyal and stood by his word? Someone Harriet could be proud to have in her family lineage?

It would take a miracle.

Harriet's phone chimed, and she drew it from her bag. A text awaited her from Eleanor Caldwell. Harriet peered at her screen.

I TOOK THE MANUSCRIPT. COME TO THE WINDSOR HOTEL IMMEDIATELY.

White Church Bay
Summer 1918

They'd failed. He had failed. His and Alice's plans to help the war effort had come to nothing.

Rhys sat on the sea wall and gazed at the placid waters, so at odds with how he felt.

Too much had changed in the last year. He hardly knew how to comprehend the difference. The bright bloom of summer overtook the coast, replacing the chill and gloom of winter. The aftermath of the train crash was mostly cleared away, and still no one knew its true cause.

Rumor blamed it on faulty track overdue for repair, though Rhys knew that was a hasty story cobbled together by the authorities. He had the date nails to prove it, but evidence didn't matter if no one wanted to hear the truth. The saboteur was long gone, so the authorities swept the matter under the rug.

Sometimes the truth was something no one could face. Rhys understood that.

The world chugged along as usual, but his life had fallen apart. The changes were insignificant to most people, but he felt the loss so keenly, it was as if a great chasm had opened in the heart of White Church Bay. A void that couldn't be filled with anything but Alice's presence.

And she was gone. Flown to the arms of heaven after a long respiratory illness brought on by the chemical leak from the cargo cars. Just as he had watched and worried over her decline soon after she started at the factory, so he fretted over the cough that began that ill-fated night the train derailed. Her progression into this final illness had rendered him completely helpless.

Different emotions warred within him. Grief as clean and sharp as the cliffside. Anger as tumultuous as a stormy sea. Bittersweet gratitude that he'd met Alice in the first place.

It was a lot to hold, but he didn't have a choice. Armed with the information Alice had given him about Hans, Rhys had scoured the track and found the loose fittings. He took them to the authorities, but everyone he encountered made it clear they wanted nothing to do with his theories about the crash. They all wanted to move on. The war wasn't over, and no one had time to dwell on a train crash in a small village. There were more important battles to fight. No one cared that Hans had escaped. No one cared that Alice had lived so courageously and died for nothing.

Rhys couldn't let it go. He owed it to Alice to honor her passing with the truth. How could he get people to listen?

Spring 1919

That spring, a newspaper advertisement delivered his answer.

Author Seeking Retreat Location
Author seeks accommodation for writing retreat.
Dates needed: April 2–May 2
Seaside preferred.

When Rhys contacted the author, Adelaide Evergreen, an idea began to form. Adelaide had fallen on hard financial times and intended to use the retreat to churn out another of the sort of stories that had previously brought her fame. But would the world fall apart with one less book of talking rabbits and inquisitive children? Rhys didn't think so. Adelaide had been part of an artists' enclave in London in her youth and hadn't been quiet with her opinions. He learned that, aside from writing children's books, she had a background writing political op-eds. She'd stopped writing those when her work was defamed as "nothing but a pack of salacious lies."

"I have a story that would put your name front and center again," he told her. "Adelaide Evergreen will be known first and foremost as a truth-teller. Your reputation would be restored."

"I am most interested," she replied.

So he'd talked her into taking the spare room in the fisherman's cottage, and in no time she had set up residence with her tattered carpetbags and eccentric ways. She scribbled from dawn to dusk then lit a candle and wrote some more. She ate little and talked even less, though he often found her wandering the village after interviewing another local connected to the crash. She took his sparse knowledge and wove it into the tapestry of her tale.

He couldn't wait for her to be finished. Finally, the truth would come out. The book would be his ode to Alice. His apology for not protecting her. The fulfillment of his promise to help.

CHAPTER TWENTY-THREE

Harriet tightened her grip on the steering wheel as she drove to the hotel. The car park by the Windsor was nearly empty when she arrived, and early afternoon sunlight glinted off the ocean. The air felt charged, as if a squall was about to blow in. She shivered as she walked to the hotel, grateful for the building's warmth when she stepped inside.

A woman sat at the front desk, and Harriet hurried toward her. Her name tag read MARLA.

"Hello," Harriet said. "I'm trying to contact someone who's staying here. Could you ring her room for me, please?"

"Do you know the room number?"

"I don't. But her name is Eleanor Caldwell."

Marla typed something on her keyboard before staring at her computer screen. Then she typed and paused again. Finally, she swiveled away from the screen to face Harriet. "I'm sorry, but there's no one staying here by that name."

"What?" Harriet scratched her head. "But that doesn't make sense." It had only been half an hour since Ellie's text.

Harriet stepped away from the desk to fish her cell phone from her purse. She dialed Ellie's number but got her voice mail.

Frustrated, Harriet returned her phone to her bag again.

Ellie was one of her allies in the beginning. But who knew what she was to Harriet now? Perhaps she was leading Harriet on another rabbit trail to a dead end.

She thanked Marla and headed for the exit.

A robust woman wearing an apron and pushing a cleaning cart stopped her. "Wait a minute, miss. Is your name Harriet?"

"Yes." Harriet froze in her tracks.

"I couldn't help but overhear you. Did you say you were supposed to meet someone named Eleanor?"

"Yes, I did."

"Here." The woman reached into her apron pocket and handed Harriet a folded sheet of paper. "I just cleaned her room. This was left on her nightstand. I think it might be for you."

Harriet unfolded the piece of paper. The Windsor Hotel's fancy letterhead graced the top, followed by a note scribbled underneath in blue ink.

> *Harriet—*
>
> *Sorry for the confusion. Meant to meet you, but I had to get back to York right away, and it couldn't wait. Just remember, you've already been where you need to go. Return there to find what's lost. Don't miss today's post.*
>
> *—Ellie*

Harriet frowned. Ellie must've been worried the message would fall into the wrong hands, to disguise the information so. "What does it mean?"

The cleaning lady shrugged and resumed her duties.

As no one else seemed to know anything about Ellie's whereabouts, Harriet tucked the paper into her coat pocket and headed outside.

"What are you up to, Ellie?" Harriet muttered as she got into her car to let the engine warm. The doctoral student's note was as mysterious as her behavior. Harriet rolled the words around in her mind. It was like a riddle. *You've already been where you need to go. Return there to find what's lost.*

Ellie had said in her original text message that she'd taken the manuscript. So her cryptic note must be referencing the document's location. Someplace that Harriet had already been.

She ran through the locations she'd visited recently. Her own house. Aunt Jinny's cottage. The museum. The veterinary clinic. Cliffside Chippy. Church. Will's home. The Cinder Track. The list was extensive.

She blew out a frustrated breath. Well, that part of the message wasn't any help at all.

She went on to the next part of Ellie's message. *Don't miss today's post.*

Today's post? Was Ellie talking about the newspaper? Or perhaps the mail? But what would that have to do with the manuscript? Harriet wasn't sure, but she did know that she couldn't figure this out on her own.

She contacted Aunt Jinny then Ashley and told them what she'd discovered. Ashley helpfully reminded her that the location list could be narrowed to places Ellie and Harriet had in common. That left…what?

Harriet had just come from the Windsor Hotel, and she knew the manuscript wasn't there. The shop where Ellie and she had talked while Ashley bought toothpaste? Unlikely. Then it hit her.

"The museum! Ash, the manuscript's at the museum." It was so obvious. Hadn't Ellie mentioned that she was concerned about taking the manuscript off the premises? She was worried over the legal ramifications of removing the document without permission. She must have decided to hide it in plain sight. Her mention of the post likely meant it was disguised as an outgoing mail package.

"I don't know if the Müellers or Robert suspect anything," Harriet continued. "But I know that Robert was onto Ellie, at least that night she was snooping at the museum. It's possible he could suspect something now."

"We have to get to the museum without rousing suspicions."

"And that's exactly why there's no *we*," Harriet said. "I need to go alone."

Ashley protested, but Harriet stood firm. "I don't think I'll be in any danger, but just to be on the safe side, I don't want anyone else there. Besides, I need you as backup. What if we need to contact the police? Who knows what might happen if the wrong person gets wind of me trying to locate the manuscript? The Müellers have already proven that they're desperate to keep their family's past secret. They've threatened and manipulated, and they've likely bribed Robert. Who knows how they got to Judith? I even wonder if they had Ellie on their side at one point."

"Okay. We'll hang back," Ashley reluctantly agreed. "But your aunt and I will be keeping close tabs on the situation."

Harriet cobbled together a hasty plan with Ashley before ending the call. She was as ready as she'd ever be.

Harriet arrived at the car park before her friends. She climbed out of her vehicle and hurried toward the museum. She wasn't sure when the mail would be picked up from the museum, but she hoped she hadn't missed it. She checked her watch. Ellie had only messaged her about the manuscript location an hour ago. Surely she still had time.

Harriet's phone buzzed from her bag, and she stopped walking to answer it. "Hello?"

"Where are you?" Polly sounded frustrated. "I expected you back ages ago."

"Long story. I'm in town, heading for the Fisherman's Lane Museum. I think I know the location of the manuscript."

"That's great, but what do I tell your clients?" Polly asked. "Your afternoon is booked solid, and Signe Larsson is here with her rabbit."

Harriet stopped in her tracks and smacked a gloved hand to her forehead. She had gotten so wrapped up in the mystery and Ellie's enigmatic message that she completely forgot about the clinic.

"Oh, Polly. I really dropped the ball." Harriet explained the situation with the manuscript as succinctly as she could. "Can you cover for me? I'll be back as soon as I possibly can. Just let everyone know there was an emergency, and I'm happy to discount services for any rescheduled appointments."

Polly agreed to smooth things over.

Harriet ended the call and continued toward the museum. She rounded the final corner, and the stone building came into view.

She sent up another prayer that God would handle the situation. She prayed that the truth would be uncovered, regardless of whether

her family was implicated. No matter what the missing chapter revealed, she wanted the truth, and that was freeing.

It left her without any ulterior motives or reasons to twist the narrative. She would follow the facts wherever they led and deal with the outcome, whatever it may be.

She reached the museum. With faith to bolster her, she took a deep breath and stepped through the front door.

The museum was eerily silent as she entered. Petra wasn't at her usual station at the welcome desk. Harriet took advantage of the situation to peer into the hallway, spotting a large stack of outgoing mail on a table. She glanced at the packages on top but didn't find any that were the right size and shape for the manuscript.

Jumbled thoughts cascaded through her mind. Had she gotten the location wrong? Had she misinterpreted Ellie's message? Or had Ellie led her down a wrong path on purpose? Harriet wasn't sure what to think or who to trust.

She started to leave, but once again, Robert appeared as an unwelcome figure at her side. "Ellie called me. I know you're after the manuscript."

Suspicion flared. Why had Ellie called Robert? Was this an elaborate trap? If so, why would Ellie tell Harriet where the manuscript was? Why not let the manuscript be destroyed or adapted or whatever it was they were doing with it?

Robert took a step closer to Harriet. "I used to think every man had a price. But now I can see I was wrong. Ellie convinced me of that."

What was he talking about? That Ellie hadn't been bought off to set Harriet up?

"The manuscript isn't here. I took it. Ellie didn't know what she was doing. She didn't know who she was dealing with. But I do."

He glanced toward the room in which he worked. Harriet followed his gaze. She had an open view of his desk, and on its surface was a mailer envelope. It was torn open, and a sheaf of papers spilled from it.

The manuscript. Robert already had it. Harriet's heart sank. She didn't know how he'd figured it out, but it couldn't be helped now. They were in a precarious situation.

She had to get to the manuscript.

Before she could second-guess herself, she darted past him into the room and grabbed it. Judging from his shocked expression, she'd caught him off guard. He obviously hadn't expected her to snatch the manuscript from under his nose.

But she no longer had the element of surprise on her side. She started to step away from him then realized he was standing in front of the office door and she was trapped.

There was only one other way out.

She clutched the manuscript to her chest and ran through the back door into the alleyway.

CHAPTER TWENTY-FOUR

Harriet nearly lost her balance on the cobblestones as Robert careened after her.

He managed to snag a corner of her coat, but she yanked free and kept running. Thankfully, her crossbody bag with her phone was strapped securely underneath.

"Stop! You don't know what you're doing!" he yelled.

She didn't answer him. She had to get away, to take the manuscript to safety. As soon as she put enough distance between her and Robert, she'd call the authorities. She just had to get to a more crowded area where he couldn't try anything.

Most people were at work, so the narrow lanes that ran between cottages and shops were empty. She zigzagged along a few paths, but Robert managed to stay on her tracks. She could tell she was gaining a lead. Though he was taller, she was quicker. She could hear him gasping for air as his feet pounded the street behind her.

"Wait, Harriet! You don't understand!" She could hear him calling after her as he fell behind. She took advantage of his slowed pace to run up some steps and duck down a side street.

Had she lost him? She huddled in the shadows and tried to gather her bearings. She carefully slipped the manuscript into her bag for safekeeping. She had to get back to the car park, where Aunt Jinny, Ashley, and Trevor waited. But her sudden flight from the museum was disorienting. Which street was she on right now? Which direction was the car park?

Before she could figure out an action plan, her phone began to ring loudly from her purse. *No, no, no…* She frantically dug for the phone. Her hiding space would be given away.

She'd barely pulled it from her purse when she heard Robert. Her reprieve had been short. He must have caught his breath sooner than she'd hoped. She didn't know if he'd heard her phone ringing, but she had to be quiet.

She silenced her ringer before glancing at the screen to see who was calling. It was Ashley. She had to take it. What if something had happened since they'd last talked? She answered the call and pressed the phone to her ear.

"Harriet? Hello? Are you there?" Ashley asked.

"Ash, make it quick," Harriet whispered into the phone.

Robert was still shouting in the distance, but she could tell he was getting closer to her location.

"What?" Ashley said. "Harriet, I can't hear you. You'll have to speak up."

Robert was too close now. She couldn't risk him hearing her talking to Ashley.

"I'll call you back."

"Did you say you'll call me back?" Ashley was practically shouting. Her voice felt so loud, Harriet worried that Robert could hear it. "I'll only be a second. Trust me, you want to hear this info. Harriet, guess who the police caught? The Müellers."

Now Harriet realized why Ashley was talking so loudly. The sound of police sirens in the background nearly drowned out her friend's voice.

"Both of them? Garrison and Petra?" Harriet asked in a low voice.

"Yes. They were trespassing on your aunt's property, and this time, we caught them in the act. Everyone's heading to the station for questioning, so we're not at the car park. Garrison has admitted that he and Petra were trying to suppress information because of their family's connection to the Millers. They don't have the manuscript though. Did you find it at the museum?"

Harriet didn't answer Ashley's question. "And Robert? What about Robert?"

"Robert?" Ashley repeated. "Oh, Robert sounds like he's bad news. According to Garrison and Petra, he's not to be trusted. He was working for them at first. He helped them make a forgery of chapter eighteen in exchange for sizable donations to his department at the university. But sometime after that, he double-crossed them. He was working with someone else too, though they aren't sure who. They think he was working with this person to sell the original manuscript illegally. He totally bamboozled everyone."

Harriet's mind spun with Ashley's new information. Could Robert be working with Ellie? Had this whole thing been an elaborate trap set up by a feverish doctoral student and a greedy research lead? The late-night museum meeting between the two of them might not have been coincidental. But why would Ellie have left the message for Harriet at the Windsor Hotel that told her where to find the manuscript? Did she want Harriet to get framed for stealing it?

A shiver went through Harriet as she heard two sets of footsteps slowly coming closer. Who was Robert working with?

It couldn't be Ellie. It just couldn't.

Ashley's voice was urgent in Harriet's ear. "Robert is dangerous, Harriet. Stay away from him. Don't believe anything he says."

Harriet glanced up to find a street marker. "Send the police to Willoughby Lane," she whispered into the phone.

"I'm sorry, Harriet. I can't hear you. Can you speak up?"

The footsteps had grown closer over the course of Ashley and Harriet's conversation, and now they sounded as if they were nearly upon Harriet. She scarcely dared breathe, much less repeat what she had said.

"Harriet? Can you hear me? Are you at the museum right now?"

Harriet pulled the phone away from her ear. An answer, even a quiet one, would give her away to Robert and whoever else was coming around the corner with him.

"Harriet, are you there? Be careful—" was the last thing Harriet heard before ending the call.

It should have made Harriet feel better knowing that Garrison and Petra were headed to the police station, but Ashley's caution that Robert was the true danger chilled her. Who knew what he might do if he found her? He'd seemed desperate to prevent her from taking the manuscript. And now that he had someone with him, the danger was even greater.

She had to get away. She slid her phone into her purse and started to run down another path when a wave of dizziness overtook her. She pressed a hand to her head. What was wrong?

Her stomach growled. She checked her watch and saw that it was nearly midafternoon. She had been so preoccupied with the mystery that she hadn't paused for lunch. And breakfast was a distant memory.

She leaned against the wall and willed the dizziness to pass.

The footsteps grew closer then stopped.

Harriet glanced up to see Robert, flanked by Pascal King. Relief washed over her when she saw that Pascal had Robert in a tight grip, preventing him from rushing at Harriet. "You are not to lay a hand on her or that manuscript. Do you hear me?" Pascal ordered.

Robert didn't heed Pascal's advice. Instead, he wrenched free from the lawyer's grip. "You must give me that manuscript!" Robert appeared half-crazed as he lunged for Harriet with wide eyes and outstretched hands.

She threw her arms up to shield her face from the attack. But nothing happened. No blow fell.

She lowered her arms and opened her eyes to see Pascal blocking Robert's reach.

"What are you doing?" Robert shoved Pascal to get him out of the way.

But Pascal shoved back. This time, Robert lost his balance and fell, hitting his head on the cobbled ground.

Harriet's pulse thrummed in her throat. She stared at Robert's splayed form. When he didn't move, she knelt to check him. He had seemed intent on doing her harm, but she didn't feel the same about him. "He's unconscious. We have to get him help."

"Of course." Pascal pulled a phone from his coat pocket and dialed. "Hello? Yes, there's been an accident. We have an injured man on..." He glanced around until he spotted the street name. "Willoughby Lane."

Pascal waited with her until emergency services arrived. By that time, Robert had started to rouse and was babbling about the manuscript again with wide eyes.

"There, now, I think you're a bit confused," one of the medics murmured to him as they loaded him onto a stretcher. "Take it easy. Everything will be all right." They carried him out of the maze of residential lanes back toward the main road, where Harriet assumed the ambulance waited.

The moment of danger past, adrenaline ebbed from Harriet, and she shivered.

Pascal glanced over at her with a look of concern. "Are you all right?"

"I'm fine." She wrapped her arms around herself to warm up. "It's been quite a day."

"You're cold. Here." Pascal shrugged off his jacket and draped it over her shoulders. Warmth radiated through her, and her heart was touched by his thoughtfulness.

"Thank you. And thank you for protecting me from Robert." She owed her well-being and the manuscript's safety to him.

"It's the least I could do. What's next?"

Harriet sighed and felt for the manuscript in her purse. "I have to go to the police station. My friends should be waiting for me there, and I need to drop off the manuscript."

Pascal's eyebrows raised. "You have the manuscript? I thought Robert was barking up the wrong tree."

"Yes. I took it from the museum today. I was afraid Robert was going to destroy it."

"I have no doubt he would have. What a close call." Pascal shook his head. "May I offer you a lift to the station?"

Harriet waved him away. "You don't need to do that."

Pascal smiled. "I'm happy to. You don't need to be driving after the ordeal you've been through."

The thought of resting while someone else took charge was appealing. The exertion of the morning combined with her lack of food for a hazy effect. She leaned on Pascal's arm as another wave of dizziness overwhelmed her. "On second thought, a ride would be nice, thank you. What were you doing in town, anyway?"

"On another errand for the estate," he answered as he helped her down the steps. "They wanted me to negotiate for the document with the museum again. When I showed up, I heard Robert shouting. I followed him to you."

"I'm glad you did."

"I am too."

Pascal escorted her to the lot and then to his car. It was an older model with a broken taillight, but it seemed reliable enough. She climbed into the passenger's side and placed the envelope with the manuscript on her lap. He started the engine and drove toward the police station.

While Pascal drove, Harriet pulled the manuscript from its sleeve. She was glad to see it again with her own eyes. Even though the train wreck happened over a century earlier, it would feel good to finally lay the past to rest. She still hadn't had a chance to read the original chapter eighteen, and this might be her only opportunity, since the document would be handed over to the authorities in a few minutes.

Pascal turned onto the street that led to the police station. Harriet located chapter eighteen and scanned it. Most of the content was the same as in the copy Robert given her. Hans Goebel was still the saboteur who engineered the train crash, but instead of Rhys Bailey profiting from the accident, Margaret and Carl Miller—also known as Greta and Karl Müeller—were named as the culprits dabbling in the black market.

Harriet finished the chapter with a sense of satisfaction and returned the manuscript to the safety of the envelope. It was as she'd thought all along. Petra and Garrison were trying to suppress information that would paint their ancestors in an unflattering light, and they'd pulled Robert into their web of lies.

Though what had Robert said when he'd chased after her and the manuscript? *You don't understand…*

She'd assumed he meant she didn't understand how the Müellers' reputation would be tarnished. How his job would be in peril. That it was better to keep things quiet and subdued.

But what if he had meant something entirely different?

She wasn't sure why a spark of doubt flickered in her mind, but it did. Something was bothering her, something about Adelaide Evergreen. She pulled the papers from her purse that she had printed at the library. She quickly skimmed Hans Goebel's obituary, noting that the man had died of advanced liver disease in the 1920s. She'd just begun scanning Adelaide Evergreen's obituary, however, when the vehicle stopped.

Harriet raised her head. Pascal's car idled on an unfamiliar stretch of road. Snow flurries blurred the view from the windshield. "Where are we?"

"There was an accident. I had to take a detour," Pascal explained. His bronzed hands rested easily on the wheel. "It seems a storm is blowing in."

It was a reasonable enough explanation, but Harriet's doubt increased. Something was wrong. Very wrong. She couldn't put her finger on what though.

She bent her head over the copies again.

> *We regret to announce that Mrs. Adelaide Evergreen-Kaplan, wife of sea captain Peter Kaplan, passed away Sunday last from consumption. Mrs. Evergreen-Kaplan was a much-loved British children's author whose work included fifteen volumes. She and Mr. Kaplan married in 1902, and the pair resided largely in Collioure until her untimely death. The couple had no children.*

Suddenly, all the disparate, fragmented clues she had been mulling over came together into one cohesive whole. Realization dawned, along with a tremor of fear.

"Adelaide Evergreen didn't have any children," she said to Pascal, trying to keep her voice level. "So how can you represent her grandchildren?"

CHAPTER TWENTY-FIVE

Pascal raised an eyebrow. "That's interesting. I'm not sure what you mean."

Harriet studied the lines of his face. The dark circles under his eyes that she'd thought were evidence of hard work and late nights. His tan skin that meant he was outdoorsy. "It's impossible."

"How so?" Pascal sounded distracted as he turned on his blinker and swerved left.

"You said you worked for Adelaide's grandchildren. It's pretty tough for someone to have grandchildren if they haven't had children first."

"Took you long enough to catch on. Not that it matters now, hmm?" Pascal's voice had changed from the gentlemanly tone she'd grown familiar with to a detached, cold one. The difference was so stark that it sent an icy chill down her spine.

Harriet refused to dignify his question with a response. "Are you even a lawyer?"

"I was." Pascal ground his teeth together. "Until my condition became prohibitive. I have dear old Great-Great-Grandfather Hans to thank for that genetic gift."

Harriet had to distract Pascal. If she could keep him talking, maybe she could manage to slip her phone from her purse. Then she could hide it under the manuscript and text Ashley.

"Your condition?" She stalled for time, piggybacking on Pascal's earlier statement.

"Hereditary liver disease." Pascal narrowed his eyes at the road in front of them. "It's incurable, and it's progressed quickly over the past few years. I had to leave my job at the firm, though Yvette did a wonderful job pretending to my receptionist, don't you think?"

"That wasn't real?"

"Of course not. She was some actress I hired."

Harriet was stunned into momentary silence.

Pascal gave her a sideways glance. "I thought you suspected something when we had lunch."

Harriet found her voice slowly. "No. I didn't suspect anything." Maybe she should have. She'd already read Alice's letters by then, and she knew about Hans's condition. But too many details had muddied the waters.

She couldn't believe she hadn't seen the truth right in front of her. But that was how things were sometimes. She hadn't wanted to cast Pascal in the role of villain. After all, he'd known her beloved uncle.

A pang coursed through her as she came to another fresh understanding. All of Pascal's attention was false as well. He hadn't thought her captivating or worthwhile. All he wanted was the manuscript. The realization added insult to injury.

She looked at her lap again. The manuscript needed to be her focus now. She had to protect it and keep it out of Pascal's hands.

Bit by bit, she began the slow process of maneuvering her phone from her purse. She needed to make a call before they got to wherever it was he was taking her. Otherwise, she might be in more danger than Adelaide Evergreen's manuscript.

Pascal drummed his fingers on the steering wheel. "Running into you was a great help, you know. I have your aunt to thank for the introduction. She was so trusting. She thought she knew me because she met me once fifteen years ago."

Harriet had managed to get her phone into her lap, hidden under the manuscript. Now to pull up the contacts. She moved her hand just enough to raise the manuscript so she could see the screen. Hopefully, Pascal was focusing enough on the road that he would ignore her.

Pascal continued. "I wondered what angle I was going to use. I was certain if I spent too much time with her, she would see through my story. But she never caught on. And neither did you. It appears I'm a pretty good liar."

A sign flashed past Harriet's window. She'd opened her message app and saw that it was open to her last conversation with Ashley. She managed to type CINDER TR and then—

"What are you doing?" He screeched the car to a halt in the middle of the road. Luckily—or maybe not—there weren't any other vehicles around. She had just enough time to push send and then the button that turned off the screen before he shoved the manuscript aside. The envelope fell to the floorboard and revealed the phone she held beneath it.

"Ah, I wondered if you would try something." Pascal grabbed her phone. "I can't get rid of you fast enough."

He pulled up to the Cinder Track museum and exited the vehicle. Harriet picked up the envelope and clutched it to her chest. She flung open the door and tried to spring out, but he was suddenly there, and he grabbed her arm. She thought about fighting him, but he was a tall, muscular man and would certainly be able to overpower her. Driving snow blinded her as he pushed her ahead of him. She stumbled and slid her way to a ramshackle cabin that she could barely see through the snow swirls.

The room was small and sparsely furnished. A suitcase lay open on the floor. This was the cabin Ashley and Trevor had found the day she'd confronted Judith here.

Pascal took off his coat and smirked. "I have to say, you aren't as bright as I thought you were. It certainly took you long enough to catch on to me. I was going to dump you on the side of the road and take the manuscript, but now I think I need a more permanent solution. You've read the manuscript. You know too much, and I have a feeling you won't be bought off like some people."

Harriet's stomach seized. "Were you working with the Müellers?" The siblings were being questioned by the police at that moment. Harriet could only hope they'd spill all their knowledge of Pascal so the authorities would know the real culprit was still at large.

"I was working with the Müellers for a while, yes. But then we stopped seeing eye to eye."

"Why?"

"All they cared about was keeping their name clean," Pascal ranted. "But they didn't care about Hans's legacy. They didn't want to edit chapter eighteen any more than they had to. They said it was an 'unnecessary risk.' Yet they were happy to take a risk to protect their ancestor."

"What about Robert? Was he working for you?" Harriet demanded. If she could stall Pascal and keep him talking, it would give the authorities more time to track her down.

"He was. Most people have their price. It just so happens that my offer was higher than the Müellers' to forge that fake chapter implicating your great-uncle or whatever he was to you." Pascal's laugh was without mirth. "At least, Robert thought it was. He was quite angry when the check I wrote him bounced."

So that must've been why Robert showed up outside Harriet's home that day, demanding Pascal's number. His payday hadn't cashed out the way he'd hoped. But that didn't explain Pascal's response to him just a few minutes ago.

"He didn't seem angry when you two found me after I ran from the museum. He seemed desperate. Why did you attack him? I thought you were protecting me at the time, but I know better now."

"He'd had a change of heart, flimsy fellow. That doctoral student got to him."

Ellie. It sounded as if she had influenced Robert in a positive way. Harriet was glad.

"Enough talking. What we need around here is fewer words."

Pascal snatched the manuscript from her then pulled something from the pocket of his coat. Harriet gasped as she realized what it was.

If she needed any more confirmation, this was it. It was him that day at the Cinder Track. The lighter Trevor had found was his.

"Many thanks for returning my lighter. Even if you didn't know it belonged to me. It's a family heirloom, you see." His smile was cruel, and she wondered how she ever found him handsome. "Hans gave it to his son, and it passed through the generations to me."

Pascal flicked his thumb across the top of the lighter and produced a flame. He moved it closer to the envelope containing the irreplaceable Evergreen manuscript.

Harriet reached out a hand. "Stop. Please."

Pascal laughed, and the sound sent a chill up her spine. He extinguished the lighter. "Do you really think I'd destroy the very thing I've been searching for since I arrived? You are so gullible. No, once I get this manuscript out of the country, I plan to sell it. It'll fetch a nice sum on the black market. Certain experimental treatments for liver conditions don't come cheap, you know. And thanks to Robert Callum, my ancestor won't be the one thrown under the bus in chapter eighteen."

He smirked as he tucked the envelope securely under one arm. "Now to take care of one final thing..."

He reignited the lighter and moved to the room's shabby curtains. This time, he touched the flame to his target. Harriet watched helplessly as flames climbed the fabric. The odor of thick smoke filled the room. She turned to the door.

"That won't do, will it?" Pascal's voice came from behind her.

The next thing Harriet knew, something hard crashed down on her head.

Then darkness.

White Church Bay
Fall 1919

By autumn it was abundantly clear that Adelaide was not well. When Rhys visited her, it grew increasingly difficult to hold a conversation. She coughed and coughed until she had to ask him to leave.

She had chosen White Church Bay in which to write because her physician thought the sea air might prove beneficial. But her heavy workload took a toll. The consumption she sought respite from worsened. It reminded Rhys of Alice.

Adelaide's retreat was soon cut short. She never finished her book. All too quickly, the author was also gone, though not dead.

She returned south to her home in the French countryside, where her sea captain husband took leave of his position to care for her. Rhys was happy she had family by her side. But he was distressed that the author's letters to him grew few and far between. Then one day he received news he didn't want to hear.

Dear Rhys,

Ever an author, I've drafted several copies of this letter. I've sent none, however, until this one. The news I must give is not what you wish to hear.

I know you said there was no rush, that I was free to return to my work after my convalescence. But time has lent me some perspective. Writing is a difficult endeavor, not for the faint of heart. This manuscript drives home that point.

I'm not a young woman anymore. I don't have the verve I once did to face critics. I have decided to abandon this project as a protective measure. You understand, I hope, my feelings on this. Even if you don't, I hope you can forgive me.

I am appreciative of the support you provided me. Please destroy the pages I left behind. I remain forever in your debt.

A. Evergreen

The letter angered him so much that he tore it to shreds. Then he burned it in the fireplace.

He couldn't bring himself to burn the manuscript as Adelaide had requested. It was his last link to Alice. His promise to her, incomplete.

CHAPTER TWENTY-SIX

Harriet awoke to the warm hazel of Will's eyes. She was inside a police car, but the driver and passenger seats were empty. Where were the officers?

"What—what happened?" She struggled to sit up, but Will held her steady.

"No, don't move. You have a head injury."

The terror of the afternoon rushed back. "Will, Pascal stole the manuscript. Then he caught the curtains on fire, and—" The situation was confusing, and it was difficult to put what had happened into words.

"Ah. I wondered what started the blaze. It's a miracle we arrived when we did. I hate to think what might've happened to you, trapped inside, if the flames had spread." His words trailed off, and a pained expression crossed his face. "Anyway, Ashley put it out in the nick of time, before anything else caught. Thank goodness Robert knew where Pascal had taken you."

"Robert?"

"Yes. He called the station from the hospital to warn them about Pascal. He told them to check the old cabin by the Cinder Track museum. Then you confirmed it with your text to Ashley. Fortunately, we were already on our way at that point, but it was good to know we were going in the right direction. Ashley was kicking herself that she didn't put two and two together earlier."

It was a lot of information to take in. Robert had sent her friends to her aid. Ellie had been right about him, and Harriet had the two of them—and Ashley—to thank for her safety.

"You sure know how to do things in style." Will smiled down at her. "A fire, a snowstorm, *and* a possible concussion?"

"You said the fire was extinguished. I didn't order the snowstorm. And I don't have a concussion. Just a—" She winced as a throbbing pain lanced through her head. "Just a slight cut."

"I'd like to make sure of that if it's all right with you." Will maintained eye contact with Harriet. Oh, those hazel eyes. How had she missed the affection in them? "Will you answer some questions so I can make sure you're all right?"

She swallowed. "Okay."

"What's your name?"

"Harriet Bailey."

"Good. And can you tell me your birthday?"

"January fourteenth."

"You're thinking clearly. Now, one last question to make extra sure." He smiled down at her. "Will you go on a date with me?"

Had she heard him right? Perhaps her head injury was worse than she'd thought. "Um, can you repeat that one? I think I misheard you."

"You didn't. I should've asked a long time ago, but I was afraid that you'd said you reciprocated my feelings at Christmas because you were being polite. Or you were reacting to your last near-death encounter—which seems to be becoming a habit, I might add. I wanted to give you the option to back out, without any pressure or obligation. I tried to test the waters with your birthday gift, but I shouldn't have been so obtuse. I should have come out and asked then."

So he *had* meant the London Symphony Orchestra tickets to be a romantic gesture. And he'd been holding back for the same reason she hadn't followed up after their conversation on Christmas Eve. Leaving friendship for uncharted territory was frightening. Yet, now, gazing into Will's eyes, feeling cared for, she felt it was worth the risk.

"Would you do me the honor of going to the Moonlit Seaside Walk with me?" he asked. "As a date, to be clear. Not as friends."

"I'd love to."

Suddenly, she was keenly aware of his warm embrace. He must've felt the tension too, because he cleared his throat and averted his gaze to the window. The sound of sirens grew louder, until finally, the car door opened, and a swirl of snow blew in.

"There's the ambulance. Off we go." He hovered nearby as the emergency techs had Harriet lie down on a stretcher so they could assess her injuries.

Harriet's mind continued to spin. What about Pascal? He had meant to leave her to who knew what outcome in the cabin. She shuddered to think what might've happened if the fire had spread or her head injury been worse.

Yet all the good outcomes in the world couldn't erase the fact that Pascal stole the manuscript. And with it the truth Adelaide Evergreen had brought to light with her writing.

Unless they could catch him…

"Wait!" she gasped, much to the confusion of the emergency tech assessing her head wound.

Will appeared at Harriet's elbow. "Hey, calm down. What's wrong?"

"Maybe we can still catch Pascal. I couldn't have been unconscious for long. He might be hiding nearby. Are the police searching for him and the manuscript?"

"They're combing the area for him right now, and I think they have a good chance of catching him. He's on foot."

"On foot? Where's his car?"

"I'm guessing his car is that beater with the broken taillight? It must have refused to start when he left you for dead. How's that for providential interference? And you don't need to worry about the manuscript."

"Will, that's the only copy in existence."

"Then it's a good thing that the police have it, isn't it?"

"I don't understand. I saw Pascal steal it."

Will shook his head. "I'm not sure what you saw Pascal take, but it wasn't the original manuscript. Robert mentioned something about making a duplicate. Does that ring a bell with you?"

"Yes, but I thought he only duplicated one chapter. Not the whole manuscript." Apparently, Robert was a more complicated figure than Harriet had realized. "Talk about a bait-and-switch. No wonder he was trying to explain when I took off with the wrong one."

Will must have seen the distress on her face. "Robert kept the original document safe. Since the manuscript was slated to go to the university, Petra had already transferred ownership of the book to him as research lead on the project. That gave him the authority to hand it over to the police as evidence. The manuscript you took from the museum, which Pascal stole from you, was a clever forgery. Don't worry about the real one. It's safe and sound with the police."

That was easy for Will to say. Harriet had experienced Pascal's single-mindedness firsthand. If he was still lurking in the area and got an inkling that the real manuscript was with the police, it could spell trouble.

"Where's the real manuscript now? Has anyone seen Pascal?" Harriet was beginning to panic. Just because it seemed as if Pascal fled the scene didn't mean he had. He might be sneaking around in the woods as he did that day at the Cinder Track.

"I don't know. I think he was gone before we got here." Will tried to soothe Harriet's frazzled nerves. "And the original manuscript is in an evidence box in the other squad car. They sent two cars. Don't worry. I'm sure the police are taking care of things."

Harriet hoped so, but she wouldn't put anything past Pascal. She strained to peer through the swirling snow from the small windows of the emergency vehicle. "What about Ashley? And Trevor? Aunt Jinny? Where are they?" She needed to know they were all safe.

"Your aunt took Trevor to her cottage, and the police gave Ashley and me a ride here. She rode in the other squad car with the manuscript. She's been handling everything with the police while I checked on you."

If Ashley and the original manuscript were both in the other squad car, that made her a target. "We need to check on Ashley. Now."

"What's going on?" he asked.

Harriet explained the situation with Pascal. He'd wounded and abandoned her in a room with a blazing fire. What if she'd been injured more severely and needed medical attention? What if she'd remained unconscious as the room caught fire? She could have died of smoke inhalation or been burned alive before help arrived.

Pascal didn't seem to care—in fact, he seemed to have set up that very situation—and his callousness made her shudder. With his lack of regard for human life, anyone could be in real trouble if they came between him and Adelaide's manuscript.

Will seemed to realize the gravity of the situation, and he immediately left to check on Ashley.

Harriet uneasily settled back onto the stretcher as the medics finished examining her head. They assured her they thought the cut wouldn't require stitches. As one of them pinched a butterfly bandage over the wound, wild shouts met Harriet's ears. "What's going on?" She feared the worst.

The medic restrained her as she tried to scoot off the gurney. "Miss, you need to lie down. You've had a head injury. Miss!"

His efforts were futile as Harriet pushed her way past him and his colleague.

She'd been right. Pascal hadn't traveled far. No wonder, with his condition and the weather. He fought against the officer who tried to restrain him, fell in the snow, and didn't stop struggling until Van warned him that everything he did after that would be charged as assault on a police officer. At that, Pascal stopped and held up his hands in surrender.

"Everything secure?" Another officer trotted across the snow to check on the situation while Van cuffed Pascal.

"Under control. I'm reading caution now." Van's voice carried to Harriet on a current of wind. "Mr. King, you do not have to say anything, but it may harm your defense if you do not mention when questioned something which you later rely on in court. Anything you do say may be given in evidence."

Ashley hurried across the snow toward Harriet as the detective constable made his arrest. “Harriet! Are you okay?”

“I could ask the same of you.”

The two friends hugged and confirmed that both of them were fine as Pascal was loaded into the police car Harriet had been in. She was relieved to see they hadn’t put him in the one with the manuscript.

Then Will followed Harriet as the emergency techs got her settled in the ambulance. He smoothed her hair back from her face. “We’ll meet you at hospital. Okay?”

“Okay.”

Harriet allowed the medics to secure her on the gurney. It took a few moments for her brain to catch up to reality. She was safe. They were all safe, and Pascal couldn’t hurt them anymore. At least, not for the immediate future. Only time would tell what punishment he would receive for his actions, though she couldn’t imagine he would get off easy.

The path to protecting the truth had been a bumpy one, but they’d finally reached the end of it.

CHAPTER TWENTY-SEVEN

The mystery finished right where it had started—in the sitting room of Aunt Jinny's cottage. The afternoon had been spent at the hospital with Aunt Jinny as supervising physician.

After she had assured everyone that Harriet's head wound was a minor one, they'd spent the rest of the daylight hours sorting out more details with the authorities. Van was giving the manuscript—the real one—a police escort to York St. John's University. Garrison and Petra Müeller faced penalties for tampering with the manuscript, but it sounded as if they and Robert were fully cooperating with the police.

Judith and Harriet made amends as well. Judith confessed to the mysterious phone calls—except for the one earlier that day, which was curious—and even stopped by the hospital with a lovely get-well bouquet that she'd assembled from her own garden.

With all those details taken care of and a hot cup of tea in her hand, Harriet was ready to sift through everything that had happened over the past two weeks.

"Let's start at the beginning." Ashley curled into an armchair. "This has been a tangled tale, and I'm still a little confused."

Harriet took a breath. "It all started when Petra read the manuscript."

"No, I mean the very beginning," Ashley interrupted. "What happened with the train crash?"

Lounging on the sofa next to her, Trevor perked up at the word *train*. "Did you figure it out?"

"Ah." Harriet took a sip of tea and readied herself for a long story. "Hans Goebel traveled from Germany to England as a wartime spy. He took a job at one of the national filling factories to gather information that might be useful and find ways to set back the Allies' efforts."

"So Alice was totally right about him," Aunt Jinny said. "I assume he caused the crash, but how?"

"He removed fittings from the track, aided in part by the Miller family, who stood to benefit heavily from the crash's aftermath. After the train crash, the Millers made their fortune on the black market and became a prominent family in White Church Bay. Hans, meanwhile, pocketed a large payday from his superiors and fled to France with his family, where he lived out his few remaining years. His liver condition wasn't the only thing he passed down, however. He also passed down a sense of bitterness and entitlement."

Aunt Jinny harrumphed. "Seems like Pascal King got the lion's share of that. I don't know how I was deceived by him, Harriet. I feel utterly responsible."

"Don't, please." Harriet hurried to reassure her aunt. "We were all taken in by him. He was a master manipulator."

"How did he get so far off track though? I didn't know him well when he was a young man, but your uncle did. Dom was an excellent judge of character. Pascal wouldn't have been able to fool him."

Harriet shrugged. "Maybe he was on the right path back then. All it takes are a few poor choices. A little bit of resentment creeping in. Before you know it, you're miles away from where you started, and even you aren't sure how it happened."

"Where does Adelaide Evergreen come into the picture?" Ashley asked. "How did she get involved?"

"Because of my great-great-granduncle Rhys. He knew what Hans was up to, thanks to Alice's letters. He scouted the track after the crash and found the loose fittings. He tried to go to the authorities, but the Millers exerted enough pressure that matters were dropped. When he saw Adelaide Evergreen's advertisement in the paper seeking a retreat location, he reached out to her. I think he hoped she would bring some legitimacy to his claims. But she got ill before she could finish the book, and his hopes were dashed."

"Until a few generations down the line." Ashley raised her eyebrows. "Which brings us to present day. Walk me through the timeline. What happened after Aunt Jinny dropped the manuscript off at the museum?"

With the history portion of the explanation done, Trevor retreated to his book, which was another thick volume on locomotives.

This was the part Harriet thought got quite interesting though. While the modern-day mystery might not feature secret spies, it did include some twists and turns.

"All right. Buckle your seat belts." Harriet adjusted her position on the other end of the sofa from Trevor. "Petra was elated when she first received the manuscript, but that all changed when she read chapter eighteen. The manuscript accused her ancestors of profiting from the crash by building their wealth on black-market activity. The new information threatened her family's legacy and all they had built over the years. I can understand why she responded the way she did."

"I can fill in here." Aunt Jinny transferred her cup and saucer to the coffee table. "Petra said some things at the station that clarified her next moves. When I told her I had a conflict with picking up the manuscript, she thought she had some time to formulate a plan. But then when Harriet showed up at the museum, she panicked. She pulled chapter eighteen from the manuscript to buy time. She just had to put us off for a while so that she could gather her bearings. Garrison offered to help her. They closed the museum for a few days to give Petra time to carry out her idea."

"Which is where Robert comes in, right?" Ashley asked.

Harriet nodded. "Exactly. Petra approached Robert about the situation and asked him to forge a copy of chapter eighteen that didn't implicate her family. When he was reluctant to keep her secret, she bribed him, offering to donate money to his department at the university if he helped her. While the museum was closed, Robert worked to create a forged chapter that would tie in seamlessly with the original manuscript. Petra also bribed him by telling him she would donate the original manuscript, with the forged chapter in place of the original, to York St. John's. Robert would have full control of it. Once it was displayed, it would be even more legitimized in the eyes of the viewing public."

A smile played on Ashley's lips. "But they didn't count on us digging, did they?"

Harriet returned the smile. "No, and they didn't count on Ellie either. The Müellers thought their plan was working until Ellie got involved. She found out about the forgery and planned to take the information to the police. But Robert caught her sneaking around before she could do that. He threatened to destroy the entire original manuscript if she didn't cooperate with him and the Müellers."

"That's awful." Aunt Jinny frowned.

"Definitely." Harriet took another sip of tea. "But Ellie was committed to protecting the truth and the manuscript. She came up with a plan to hide it in plain sight. She sealed it in a mailer addressed to the university, so if it had actually been mailed, she would have a chance to intercept it. With the number of packages coming and going from the museum every day, no one noticed another envelope in the mail room's outbox. It was a clever way to keep the manuscript under the radar while everyone was searching for it."

Aunt Jinny's brow wrinkled. "But why not take it to the police at that point? Why jump through hoops to keep the manuscript hidden?"

"Because Ellie learned about Pascal's involvement," Harriet explained. "She knew that Pascal approached Robert and offered him more money than the Müellers had, if Robert would give Pascal the manuscript. She feared that, with both men working together, she was fighting a losing battle to get the manuscript to the authorities. The stakes were too high for her to risk actually trying to take it out of the building. Robert had already threatened to destroy the document if she didn't cooperate."

"I get it," Ashley said. "But why didn't anyone suspect that Ellie took the manuscript? Didn't the museum have security cameras? You said Petra accused you of taking the manuscript because you were on the security footage."

"That was all Robert's doing," Harriet answered. "He disarmed the security cameras in his office Sunday evening so no one would overhear his negotiations with Pascal. That meant there was no video footage of him, but it also meant there was no footage of Ellie either. Because nearly everyone associated with the mystery was doing underhanded things to hide the truth, the Müellers assumed I was doing the same. They accused me of stealing the manuscript because I was in the museum the day Petra noticed the manuscript was missing."

"And Judith went along with them because she was upset at how she thought Rhys treated Alice?" Aunt Jinny suggested.

"Precisely."

"Why was Robert fooled?" Ashley pursed her lips. "He was watching Ellie closely. He must have known she'd done something with the manuscript. Why go along with the ruse that Harriet took it?"

"Because he needed the distraction." Harriet took another sip of tea. It had grown lukewarm over the course of their conversation. She would need to reheat it soon, but they were so close to the end of the story. "The Müellers thought he was still working for them. They had no idea of his negotiations with Pascal, and he needed things to stay that way. After all, if he could bilk two groups out of their money by pulling a bait-and-switch, he could pocket twice the profit."

"I thought he only forged chapter eighteen," Aunt Jinny said.

"At first, he did. The forged chapter that implicated Rhys Bailey would satisfy the Müellers' requests perfectly. But that left the original chapter eighteen shoved in a drawer somewhere, gathering dust. When Pascal showed up and began poking around, Robert saw an opportunity. If he could sell the real chapter eighteen to Pascal, who wanted to destroy it because of the unflattering light in which his ancestor was portrayed, he could profit even more."

"Ellie stealing the original document in its entirety blew that plan out of the water, though, didn't it?" Aunt Jinny suggested.

"It sure did. So Robert tried to pass off the forged chapter eighteen to Pascal instead."

"And Pascal got angry when he figured out it was fake and wrote Robert a bad check in return," Ashley finished. "That's why Robert was so upset the night he showed up here demanding Pascal's number. He hadn't gotten his money."

Harriet nodded. "And in the meantime, Robert's attitude toward Pascal soured. I think he finally realized money is a fickle master to serve. Ellie took advantage of the situation to talk to Robert about the right thing to do. I don't know how she did it, but he offered to help her keep the manuscript safe until they could get Pascal off the trail."

"It sounds like we owe Ellie a lot," Ashley said. "Without her, the manuscript may have been lost forever."

Harriet's cell phone began ringing from its place on the coffee table. She glanced at the screen. "Speaking of Ellie." She swiped to accept an incoming video call. "Perfect timing, Ellie." Harriet was delighted to see her friend show up on the screen. Ashley was right. If not for Ellie, the manuscript might have been lost forever and Pascal might have succeeded in his heinous plans.

"I wanted to check in on you," Ellie said. "I heard about everything that happened today. I'm so glad everyone's all right."

"We are too. All's well that ends well, and we owe a lot of that to you."

Ellie waved off Harriet's praise. "It's my responsibility to protect historical documents."

"Perhaps, but you went above and beyond," Harriet insisted. "A piece of history would be lost if it hadn't been for you. But there's something I don't understand. Why did Robert switch the fake manuscript for the original in the envelope on his desk?"

"That was one last bait-and-switch courtesy of Robert." Ellie smiled in triumph. "The final alliance Robert made was with me. I talked him into helping me keep the original manuscript safe. He anticipated that Pascal would return to the museum to take the manuscript. So he forged a hasty recreation of the rest of the document and substituted it for the original I had put in the envelope. That's what you stole from Robert's desk, and that's what Pascal tried to flee with. I'm sure Robert will face some heat for what he did. Bribery is a serious offense. So is forging. But it might work in his favor that he saved the manuscript in the end. It's never too late to do the right thing."

"What a whirlwind." Harriet pressed a hand to the bandage on her forehead.

"I'll say," Ellie agreed. "I don't know if this is the proper time to announce this, but I'd love to share my good news with you."

"Of course. Good news is always welcome," Harriet replied.

"I finally finished my thesis and submitted it. That's why I left town so abruptly. I couldn't wait to turn it in. I knew you'd figure things out with my note. You didn't need me." To say Ellie was beaming was an understatement. "Now I just have to bite my nails until my doctoral dissertation defense."

"Congratulations. That's wonderful. I'm sure all your hard work and late nights will pay off." Harriet grinned. Soon, she hoped to call her friend Dr. Eleanor Caldwell. It looked like protecting the past had granted Ellie a bright future, and Harriet couldn't be happier about it.

CHAPTER TWENTY-EIGHT

Aunt Jinny was of the opinion that Harriet should stay home and rest for another day following the incident, but Harriet wanted nothing more than to get back to normal life and put the whole situation with Pascal behind her. The man had been caught in a cavalcade of lies and would likely be going to jail for a long time.

Harriet got dressed for a day of work at the clinic and showed up to a stack of notes from Polly.

"These are the rescheduled appointments from yesterday, and here are some phone messages," Polly said around a yawn.

Harriet accepted the messages then eyed her assistant. If Polly was as tired as she was, she would welcome a sugar boost. Harriet had picked up some extra jelly beans at the store when she'd fetched candy for Trevor. She removed a packet of them from her bag and slid it across the counter. "Delivery for Polly Thatcher. Do you accept?"

Polly took the candy with a smile. "Gladly. But I might need more than one packet to get through this appointment backlog."

"Got you covered." Harriet opened her bag to reveal a large stash of candy.

"Good." Polly nodded past Harriet toward the front door. "Because I think our first client is here."

Back to business. Harriet followed Polly's gaze to see Signe Larsson entering the clinic with a small crate in her hand. It felt as if more than two weeks had passed since Oliver had come by with Lilla. Apparently, there was still a problem.

"What happened to you?" Signe frowned in concern.

Harriet's hand flew to the butterfly bandage on her head. "It's a long story."

"I hope everything is all right. Is this why you weren't at the clinic yesterday?" Signe asked.

"It is, and everything has worked out." Thanks to the friends who had rallied around her.

Harriet only hoped she could count Signe Larsson among that same community of friends. She wasn't looking forward to telling the woman that her beloved pet had a mystery illness.

"I'm glad to hear all is well." Signe got straight to the point. "Oliver told me that he brought Lilla in last week. She's still blue. Will you look at her again, please?"

Harriet nodded. "Bring her on into the exam room, and I'll take another look at her."

When they got to the exam room, Signe opened the crate and brought Lilla out. "Lilla is my first English Angora," she said as Harriet examined the rabbit. "So I don't know much about what can go wrong. Other than this blue color, she seems to be in perfect health."

While she was speaking, the events of the past week suddenly flew through Harriet's mind.

What if Lilla was suffering from a hereditary condition, just as Pascal had inherited a liver condition from Hans? Harriet handed

Lilla back to Signe, excused herself, and hurried to her office. She pulled up information on Lilla's breed, skimming the details as quickly as possible. She stopped when she reached a series of photos showing coloration differences between juvenile and adult rabbits. The patterns in the pictures exactly matched those on Lilla. Nothing was wrong with her.

When she returned to the exam room, Signe asked, "Should I put her back in her crate, or do you need to look at her again?"

Harriet pointed to the crate. "You can take her home," she said. "Lilla is in the clear. There's nothing wrong with her. Nothing at all."

Signe gaped at her. "Then what's causing the blue on her fur?"

Harriet smiled. "Her genes. She's a blue tort, or tortoiseshell. That's the type of color variation she's inherited from her parents." Harriet pulled out her phone and showed Polly the webpage she had found with pictures of juvenile English Angora rabbits. "See? The bluing of her fur matches the typical patterns a young Angora would have as she matures into an adult."

"That's great news." Signe beamed.

Harriet agreed. Sometimes the truth brought hard discoveries to light, and sometimes it was a wondrous surprise.

After all the excitement of the past few days, Harriet was ready for a relaxing evening at home. Ashley and Trevor's visit was drawing to an end, and they were scheduled to fly out on Monday. Wind rattled the windowpanes, so Harriet made a big pot of minestrone soup, and they ate at the coffee table while playing a board game.

"My guess is the gardener in the museum with the hedge clippers?" Ashley raised her eyebrows from across the table.

"Very funny." Harriet eyed Ashley's peacock-blue pawn on the board.

Trevor squinted. "Mom, there isn't even a gardener in the game. Or a museum. And definitely no hedge clippers."

Ashley blew out a breath. "I know. But there is in real life. I can't believe Pascal King turned out to be the worst of the bad guys."

It was tough for Harriet to believe as well. She had let her loneliness and hurt feelings maneuver her into a dangerous place. The outcome would serve as a reminder in the future to see the truth beyond her own desires. Thankfully, things had turned out well, and she knew God had a better plan in mind for her, even if she wasn't quite sure what it was yet.

"Is it my turn yet?" Trevor reached out for his game piece on the board. "Dad loved board games. Remember, Mom? He always used to say, 'Why do they call them bored games if they aren't boring?'"

Harriet thought the memory might coax a smile from Ashley, but instead, she sprang to her feet so quickly that she nearly upset her soup bowl and fled from the room.

Trevor looked down at his own meal. In a voice so low Harriet could hardly hear him, he said, "I really miss him. You're her best friend. Do you think she'll ever talk about him again?"

Harriet got to her feet. She was Ashley's friend and, according to Trevor, her best friend. She owed it to Ashley to be there for her when she was hurting. Sometimes best friends dug a little to reveal the truth. A temporary hurt now might help Ashley's healing in the long run.

"I'll be right back." She walked into the guest room where Ashley had disappeared. Ashley wasn't in the room, though Harriet could hear the tap running behind the closed bathroom door. It sounded as if Ashley was crying.

"Ash? Do you want to talk?" Harriet called softly, but Ashley didn't answer. Maybe she hadn't heard her.

Harriet opened her mouth to ask again when she spied Ashley's leather travel journal splayed open on the nightstand. Harriet couldn't resist. After all, her friendship with Ashley could hang in the balance. She had to know why her friend had cut off contact. Why she'd made a spontaneous trip to England to see Harriet yet wouldn't talk to her about anything of substance.

She walked across the room and reached for the journal then stopped. She couldn't do it. As anxious as she was to mend her relationship with Ashley, this wasn't the way. The ends didn't justify the means, and her interference in this way would only serve to put a wedge between her and her friend.

Unfortunately, that was the exact moment Ashley decided to exit the bathroom. "What are you doing?"

"I know this looks bad, but I didn't snoop, Ash. Honest." Harriet held up her hands. "I thought about it, but then I decided if you wanted to tell me the truth, you would."

To Harriet's surprise, Ashley crossed the room and picked up the journal. Then she handed it to Harriet. "You're right. Here."

Harriet took the book from Ashley and slowly flipped through it. Strangely, two styles of handwriting filled the pages. One she recognized as Ashley's. The other wasn't familiar. She looked up with a question in her eyes.

"It's Jon's handwriting," Ashley explained. "This was his old journal. I found it after he—after he died."

It was the first time Harriet had heard her friend acknowledge what had happened.

Ashley kept speaking. "It's a strange thing, to read someone's innermost thoughts after they're gone. It's a gift, in a way, like meeting him all over again. This is how I found out that he had a lifelong dream to visit England."

"Is that why you came here?"

Ashley nodded. "It felt like a way to say goodbye to him but also a way to celebrate him, you know? He never got to travel overseas, but Trev and I have been able to do that for him. It feels meaningful."

"That's a beautiful way to honor his memory. But why not tell me that?" Harriet frowned. "You didn't even invite me to the funeral, Ash. Did I do something to offend you?"

Ashley's eyes widened. "Of course not."

"Then why did you cut me from your life? Why did you stop confiding in me? I thought we were friends."

"We were. I mean, we are. That's not why I stopped talking to you. I avoided calling you because—" She stopped then swallowed hard, her eyes filling with tears. "Because I knew that when I told you, it would be real. I couldn't skate by on the surface of my emotions with you like I was doing with everybody else. Then the time stretched out, and before long I realized I'd missed my chance. I've treated you horribly, and I wouldn't blame you if you didn't consider us friends anymore, but—"

"Oh, Ashley." Harriet grabbed her friend's hand, her heart aching. "I'm here for you. We're always friends, no matter what."

"Thank you," Ashley whispered. "I miss Jon so much, Harriet. It feels like forever since I've heard his voice. It's as if there's this huge hole in my heart, and I don't know how to make it stop hurting."

Ashley broke down into tears, and as tough as it was to see her friend in emotional pain, Harriet could tell this was a healing type of hurt. She put her arms around Ashley and held her tight. She knew Ashley didn't need words from her at the moment. Her old friend simply needed her presence.

"Mom? Is everything okay?" Trevor appeared in the doorway with a concerned look on his face. "I'm sorry I hurt you with what I said about Dad. I just miss him."

"You didn't do anything wrong, sweetheart. It's good for you to talk about him. That's how we keep him with us." Ashley motioned him over and folded him into her arms.

Harriet wiped tears from her own cheeks as she witnessed the embrace. It had taken a trip across the ocean for Ashley to process her pain, but now at last, her healing could begin.

CHAPTER TWENTY-NINE

White Church Bay
Fall 1919

Back at the seawall once again. As the stormy tumult of waves eventually calmed, Rhys's anger at Adelaide Evergreen eventually calmed.

He sent more letters after her final one, but she never replied. His hands were tied regarding the manuscript. What recourse did he have? He couldn't solicit to have it published without her consent. He was ignorant of the process and had none of her connections.

So, after some time passed, he finally acknowledged his own helplessness. He had power in many situations, but this was not one of them.

He had to give the situation over to God.

He turned his back on the ocean, and instead, gazed inward at the land. Later generations counted on him. It was a weight he felt keenly.

He didn't intend to let them down. He would forge ahead, doing the best he could on this new course he could never have anticipated. He would rise to the level which Alice had believed him capable.

He might be alone, but he wasn't abandoned. Even if his plans hadn't worked out. The One who controlled the lilt of the sea and the position of stars in the sky still had a purpose for his life. A track to follow.

Rhys would stay focused on Him and let Him lead.

"Beautiful evening for a first date, aye?" Will asked.

First date. It still felt surreal, and look how handsome he was. He appeared every inch the Austen hero with his hazel eyes and his high-collared black overcoat. They were even walking along the shore together, for goodness' sake. All they needed to complete the image was for her to tumble from the seawall and for him to save her.

Not that she was about to do that. The ocean was at its most frigid this time of year. Such a plan would sooner catch her a case of pneumonia than someone to court her.

"Yes, it's a lovely evening. I've never seen the sky so clear and the sea so calm."

"It's as if the event were tailor-made by God himself." Will smiled then looked oddly sheepish. "I have something to confess."

"Please." Harriet held her hands up in a gesture of mock surrender. "I don't think I can take any more dramatic reveals."

"Don't worry," Will assured her. "This confession will set your mind at ease."

"All right. Tell away."

"I was the person who called you on Thursday."

"You?" Harriet felt her brow pinch into a furrow.

"Yes. The truth is, I wanted to invite you to the Moonlit Seaside Walk long before I actually did. I picked up the phone several times but never went through with it. I'm sorry if you thought the person on the other end of the line had ill intent."

Of course. It all made sense now. The dog barking in the background on that call wasn't Magnus. It was Chelsea Ward's mastiff, Bruiser. "I'm sorry I was so harsh during the call. I thought it was another prank."

Will laughed. "Well, technically, you were talking to Judith Martin."

Harriet felt herself blush. "Obviously, I was wrong about that."

"I hope you're glad I finally asked you out." Will was suddenly serious, and his eyes held hope. "The reason I hesitated for so long was because I didn't want to jeopardize our friendship."

Harriet swallowed, feeling bold after his confession of vulnerability. "I felt the same way. But to answer your question, yes. I'm incredibly glad you asked me out."

A slow grin spread across Will's face. Happiness made him even more handsome. "Then may I propose the start of a new chapter? One in which we are more than friends?"

She felt a smile tug at the corners of her lips. "I like the sound of that, sir."

"Then we're agreed." Will offered her his arm like an old-fashioned gentleman.

She looped her arm through his, and together they walked along the beach for some time, talking and getting to know each other better. He told her how he'd been obsessed with cricket as a boy and still enjoyed playing a game or two, and she told him how she had considered a career as a wildlife photographer before she realized she wanted to follow in her grandfather's footsteps and become a veterinarian. They bonded over their mutual distaste for Scotch eggs, a UK delicacy that involved a hard-boiled egg wrapped in ground sausage, coated in breadcrumbs, and deep-fried, then usually served cold. The evening was one of the loveliest Harriet could recall.

Harriet let go of Will's arm as they entered a rocky portion of the cove and put her hands out for balance so she wouldn't trip. Thank goodness she had worn her waterproof boots and warmest coat. Their view of the coastline was somewhat abbreviated here, but their position south of the main group allowed for an uninterrupted view of the sea and stars.

She thought they were alone until she heard voices even farther down the coast than where Will and she were. She stepped out of the cove to see who was speaking. The bright, unclouded moon lent plenty of light.

"It's Van and Polly," she told Will, who was peering down the shoreline as well. She started to call out to Polly to see if they wanted to walk together, but Will pulled her back.

"Wait," he cautioned.

Harriet was thankful for his advice when she saw Van take Polly's hands in his own before dropping to one knee in the sand. Then he let go to fish in his coat pocket for a box, which he opened and held up to Polly.

"He's proposing," Harriet whispered. "What do we do?"

Will didn't seem as taken aback by the whole event as Harriet did. "I suppose we stay right here. They can't see us. I don't want to interrupt their moment, and it'll be spoiled if we go out there now. After he's asked and she's accepted, we can act as if we were casually strolling down the beach the whole time. What do you think?"

"All right." As far as impromptu plans went, it wasn't bad. After Polly accepted, they could celebrate with her.

But would Polly accept? The question flew into Harriet's mind. Will seemed certain of Polly's answer, but Harriet wasn't sure. Polly had been worried over Van's odd behavior lately and had seemed relieved when he'd asked her to be with him the Moonlit Seaside Walk. But the pair had only been dating for four months.

Harriet held her breath as she waited for Polly's happy laugh and a subsequent engagement. But the only sound that met Harriet's ears was the lapping sound of water on the shoreline.

Then she heard crying, and not the happy kind.

She peeked around the rocks.

Polly's hands shielded her face as she cried, and Van rose to his feet. Even from a distance, Harriet could see the pant leg he'd been kneeling on was soaked. He was likely freezing, poor man.

Polly probably wasn't faring any better. Her voice, broken by sobs, carried on a small gust of wind. "I'm not ready for marriage… too soon…so sorry, Van…"

Van reached for her hands again. It looked like he was trying to talk to her, but Polly broke away from him and took off in the opposite direction down the shore. After a long wait, Van followed, but it was clear he wasn't pursuing her. His shoulders slumped in defeat.

Harriet shivered. The whole night had been so perfect. Until this.

She caught Will's eyes and noticed that he was affected too. "What happened?"

"I honestly don't know." Will shook his head. "I truly thought she'd accept."

Harriet let out a shaky breath. A sudden tremor of fear worked its way through her body. She had thought Polly and Van were a solid couple. If their relationship could be gone in an instant, what did that say for her and Will? They didn't have the same shared history or culture. What if things with Will never progressed beyond one date?

She had to get something off her chest, or it would haunt every minute she spent with him. "Can I ask you a question?"

"Certainly."

"What about Chelsea Ward?" Harriet stepped back so that Will's face was in light, not shadow. "I halfway thought you fancied her."

"Oh no." His face flushed. "I mean, she's a nice lass, and she's helped the parish tremendously since she got involved, but no. I helped her with Bruiser because I thought it might please you."

Relief coursed through Harriet, and the light tone the two of them had cultivated before Polly and Van's proposal returned.

The walk ended far too soon, and people started to leave the beach. Will walked a little ways ahead, and Harriet lingered for a moment at the seawall. The stars were laid thickly across the heavens, and the lull of the ocean's waves provided a wonderful lullaby.

She would need to console Polly soon. And things would be awkward with Van for a while. But for this moment, she wanted to be present with the gratitude she had for her own blessings.

She sent a prayer of gratefulness out into the vast expanse. *Thank You, Lord. Thank You for showing me the truth. Thank You for directing my paths and leading me in the direction You want. Thank You for closing the wrong doors. Thank You for this place and these people who feel like home.*

Home. Less than a year ago, she hadn't known if she could ever feel that way about White Church Bay. She'd thought she'd always be an outsider, lingering in the shadow of her larger-than-life grandad. Yet now, even with a long way to go, she could tell she was headed in the right direction. Above her, a star twinkled as if it were winking at her.

Yes, she was on the right track.

FROM THE AUTHOR

Dear Reader,

Every night before I go to bed, I step outside to feed the stray marmalade cat who has adopted my family as his own. I am often struck at these times by the beauty of the night sky, and I take a few seconds to search for the North Star. I like to recall countless travelers navigating by its steadfast compass for thousands of years.

The North Star is something we also need in our modern lives. Maybe you've experienced decision fatigue at some point in your personal life. Goodness knows we all face lots of choices in any given day. Blue shirt or black? Cream or sugar? Coffee or tea? Highway or scenic route? Sometimes choices offer even more of a challenge. This church or that one? This job or another?

If you begin to feel paralyzed by the choices before you, I want to encourage you to follow the truth that only God can provide. He is our North Star. Follow Him, and He will make all your paths straight.

Keep reading,
Shaen Layle

ABOUT THE AUTHOR

Shaen Layle is a *USA TODAY* Bestselling author and Carol Award semi-finalist who writes inspirational cozy mysteries from her home in the Midwest, where she lives with her artist husband, Danny, their two rambunctious but adorable boys, and their shelter pup, Violet. Trained as a literary novelist and with a decade of librarianship under her belt, Shaen loves discussing all things bookish with her readers on her website and on social media.

A STROLL THROUGH THE ENGLISH COUNTRYSIDE

Did you know that England has well over a hundred maintained railways that carry approximately thirteen million passengers a year? They offer a particularly lovely way to view the English countryside when visiting on holiday. However, what do you do if you'd like to tour the famed Scarborough & Whitby Railway, which ran from 1885 until 1965, when it closed to passengers?

Thanks to local preservation efforts, you can still visit the S&W Railway, if you don't mind traveling on foot or by bicycle. The Cinder Track, so named because its track ballast is composed of cinders rather than crushed stone, spans the entire thirteen-mile length of the line. The scenic terrain offers breathtaking views of the ocean and provides amateur historians plenty of fodder for discussion, as a large amount of antique track and signage remains. Several station buildings along the route have also been converted into holiday rentals for tourists. Add in some fish and chips from a local restaurant, a paperback mystery, and a hot cuppa for a charming dip into history and a vacation from everyday life.

YORKSHIRE YUMMIES

Winter Fruit Pie

And now you can see Aunt Jinny's secret ingredient—star anise!

Ingredients:

2 refrigerated premade piecrusts
½ teaspoon candied orange peel, optional
3–4 pears, ideally a cooking variety like Bosc, peeled and cut into 1-inch cubes
¼ cup brown sugar
1½ tablespoons honey
1 tablespoon water
1 star anise, or ¼ teaspoon anise seed
¼ teaspoon ground cardamom
¼ teaspoon ground ginger
¼ teaspoon ground cinnamon
Pinch of kosher salt
½ lemon, juiced
Egg wash
Sugar for dusting

Directions:

Preheat oven to 375°F.

Grease pie dish with butter and then dust with flour. Press first piecrust into bottom of baking dish. Cut off any excess on edges.

Evenly distribute candied orange peel over crust. Cook in oven for ten minutes.

While crust is cooking, make your filling by combining pear pieces, brown sugar, honey, water, star anise, spices, salt, and lemon juice in large pot. Cook over medium-high heat, stirring occasionally, until mixture thickens to syrupy consistency. This will take approximately 25 to 30 minutes. If mixture does not thicken, mix ½ teaspoon cornstarch with cool water then add cornstarch mixture to hot pear mixture. Boil for one minute while stirring. Remove star anise. Let pear mixture cool slightly.

Fill parbaked crust with cooled pear mixture. Place second piecrust over filling. Crimp edges as desired. Brush top crust with egg wash and sprinkle lightly with sugar.

Bake pie until pastry is browned, approximately 30 minutes.

Remove pie from oven and allow to cool slightly before slicing and serving.

Serve with tea and enjoy your winter treat!

Read on for a sneak peek of another exciting book in the Mysteries of Cobble Hill Farm *series!*

Wolves in Sheep's Clothing

BY SANDRA ORCHARD

"My Yorkshire puddings always deflate," Harriet Bailey lamented to her patient neighbor, Doreen Danby, in Doreen's large farmhouse kitchen early Sunday evening. In the months since Harriet arrived from the US to take over her grandfather's veterinary practice, Doreen had helped her navigate traditional UK cuisine and so much more. Today they planned to tackle the temperamental pudding. "I don't know what I'm doing wrong."

"It happens to the best of us, dear." The corners of Doreen's eyes crinkled with amusement.

Harriet had begged for advice after making a flop of the ones she'd baked for Will last week in honor of the UK's national Yorkshire Pudding Day, celebrated on the first Sunday of February every year.

Doreen peeked at the batter Harriet was still whisking. "Don't worry. With my tips, your puds will retain all their puffed-up glory. First thing to remember is to chill your batter before baking."

Doreen's eleven-year-old son, Randy, raced into the kitchen. "Is supper almost ready?"

"Not for an hour. Did you boys make sure the gates were latched properly after you checked the flock?"

"Aye." Randy eyed the platter his mom was filling with pickles.

Lowering her voice, Doreen asked Harriet, "Did you hear that another three ewes went missing yesterday? From the Huckaby place this time." She tsked. "Farmers can never afford to lose stock. But to lose ewes in lamb in this economy..." Doreen shook her head. "And one of them was their blue-ribbon winner, no less. They're fortunate the entire flock didn't follow the trio out."

Harriet flinched. She'd visited the Huckaby farm yesterday morning. What if she'd been the one who failed to secure the gate properly? She'd promised herself that she'd double-check every gate she passed through after the Trussels' ram escaped soon after she'd attended that farm. And she'd warned her intern to do the same. But if she was second-guessing herself, her clients probably were too.

"No one has spotted the ewes wandering about?"

"Nay." Doreen shooed Randy away. "If you boys are done with your chores, go finish your board game with Ava and Ella. They should be done setting the dining room table by now."

"Okay." Randy snagged a pickle on his way out of the kitchen.

Harriet chuckled at Doreen's eye roll. "You must have to cook nonstop to keep your brood full." Doreen and her husband, Tom, had five children ranging in age from five to sixteen. And every time Harriet visited, the kitchen smelled divine, thanks to Doreen's baking expertise.

"I love it." Her friend's voice exuded joy. "But with our farm-tour plans for the school's half-term break next week, mealtimes will be crazier than ever around here."

The reminder of the lengths to which so many farmers had to go to keep their farms viable pricked Harriet with another dose of guilt. If she was responsible for costing the Huckaby family three of their best ewes, she'd also cost them the lambs the ewes were expecting. Shutting down the thought before her fretting spoiled her visit with Doreen, Harriet slid the bowl of batter into the fridge and turned her full attention to Doreen's explanation of their plans.

Harriet shook her head in wonder. Lambing was already a hectic time for sheep farmers. Adding educational entertainment for tourists to their to-do list was a huge undertaking. "Maybe I should feature you in the article I've been asked to write."

"Article for what?"

"An American veterinary magazine. I occasionally submitted articles to it when I lived Stateside. Now that I'm practicing here, they've asked me to write something for their international feature. Usually, the articles contrast the veterinary practices of the featured country with the US. But I've proposed writing about how farmers are diversifying revenue streams to supplement their farm income."

"Is that so different than a Montana rancher converting his spread into a dude ranch? Or the B&Bs and 'glamping' cabins that farmers rent to tourists?"

"I suppose not." Harriet sighed. "I'd like to find a uniquely Yorkshire hook for my article though."

"I'll give it some thought and let you know if I come up with any ideas."

"Thank you." Harriet wiped down the counter where she'd been working. "By the way, the outdoor play area Tom built for the tourists looks great. The wash station is a fabulous addition. Will you allow visitors in with the newborn lambs?"

"No. We don't want to upset the new mamas. We usually have to hand-rear a dozen or so lambs every year, though, so in those cases, we might let visitors help bottle-feed them."

Harriet nodded. It wasn't uncommon for ewes with twins to not have enough milk.

"Besides seeing newborn lambs, the children can have a pony ride and pet and feed the goats, rabbits, and cow."

"Not the alpacas?" Harriet teased. Alpacas weren't always as amiable as they were cute, often seeing unfamiliar living things as a threat rather than a potential friend.

Doreen chuckled. "Tom built a second fence around the alpaca pen so young'uns can get close enough to admire them without touching them. Of course, if the littlest ones are anything like our Terrance, they'll be more interested in playing with the toy tractors in the big sandpit than anything else." She opened the oven door and checked the temperature of her roast beef then pricked a couple of potatoes and carrots with a fork. Seemingly satisfied, she removed the roasting pan from the oven. "Traditionally, we use pan drippings to bake our Yorkshire puds, but we'll save this for gravy and use lard tonight." She raised the oven temperature and retrieved a couple of muffin tins from the cupboard. "Add a half teaspoon of lard to each cup, then we'll put them in the cooker to heat."

Harriet did as instructed while Doreen transferred her roasted vegetables to heated bowls and drained the pan drippings for gravy.

By the time the rest of the meal was sorted, the oven had reached the higher temperature, and Doreen set the muffin tins inside. "You want to heat the fat in your muffin tins until it's smoking hot before you add your batter."

Harriet cringed, remembering how, thanks to an emergency vet call, she'd once forgotten about her tins in the oven. Thankfully, the blaring smoke alarm alerted her before she'd made it out the door. This time, she kept a close eye on the situation. When Doreen agreed the fat was hot enough, Harriet quickly poured the chilled batter into each cup.

"Now"—Doreen dried her hands on a tea towel as Harriet closed the oven door—"don't open that door again until they're done, or your puds will sink."

"But how will I know when they're done if I can't look at them?" Harriet squinted through the oven's window, an option she didn't have with her grandad's old stove. But even with a window, it would be difficult to tell.

Doreen set the timer. "They should be done when this goes off. Ideally, we want to see at least a ten-centimeter rise and a golden-brown crispy exterior."

Harriet was still getting used to the metric system, but she remembered enough about conversions to know that ten centimeters translated to about four inches. "How do you keep them from sinking once you take them out of the oven?"

"Keep them away from drafts and serve them as soon as possible." Doreen patted Harriet's arm. "But don't sweat it if they collapse. They'll still taste great. We are home cooks, my dear. No one expects perfection or professionalism. If they did, they could go pay for it."

"We're here." Harriet's aunt Jinny, who lived in the dower cottage next to Harriet's house, came in the kitchen door.

"We?" Harriet tilted her head to peek past her aunt. Her uncle had passed away several years ago, and if Aunt Jinny had started dating, she hadn't breathed a word to Harriet.

Aunt Jinny ushered in their handsome pastor, Fitzwilliam Knight.

Harriet's heart jolted. She hadn't told anyone other than Polly and Aunt Jinny that she and Will had started dating. Well, tried to start. So far, they'd canceled more dates than they'd managed to keep, thanks to frequent veterinary or parishioner emergencies. Will had gamely accompanied her on a couple of farm calls that had usurped their plans, but offering to reciprocate on his emergency calls hadn't felt appropriate. If someone needed him, they usually required his discretion as well.

"I'd planned to invite Pastor Will to our Yorkshire Pudding Day celebration last week, but then Tom and I came down with that nasty cold the kids brought home from school," Doreen explained, clearly unaware that Will had celebrated the occasion—over thoroughly sorry puddings—with Harriet.

His hazel eyes twinkled. "I hear Harriet is tonight's guest cook in that department."

She smoothed the fine hairs around her face that had worked free of the braid she'd put in before starting. "Yes, and I hope your expectations aren't too high. I haven't yet managed to make a single batch that didn't sink."

Will laughed, a hearty, friendly sound that warmed Harriet to the tips of her toes. "My dad says they hold more gravy that way."

Will's good-natured response dispelled Harriet's nerves. Realizing she was standing there grinning at him like a starry-eyed schoolgirl, she busied herself cleaning the mixing bowl.

Terrance, Doreen's youngest boy, raced into the kitchen, almost knocking Aunt Jinny off her feet. "Dr. Bailey, Dad wants you to come quick."

Doreen squatted in front of her son and grasped his arms. "What's happened?"

"Missy is having her baby, but it's got too many legs."

Harriet had already shed her apron and grabbed her jacket from the back of the kitchen chair. "I'll see to it," she assured Doreen. "I'll leave you to make sure those Yorkshire puddings don't sink."

Harriet found Tom in the Danbys' maternity barn.

"Am I ever glad to see you," Tom said, the relief palpable in his voice. "She's got twins jostled about in there and near as I can tell, one is trying to push its leg out at the same time as the other's head."

Harriet immediately crouched, heedless of her good trousers, next to the bawling ewe. She whispered reassurances to the distressed mama as she assessed the situation. "It's difficult to tell which leg belongs to which lamb."

Harriet managed to push back the head of the lamb that was determined to be first, enough to untangle its legs from those of its siblings. "Actually, she's carrying three lambs."

"Three?" Eager anticipation punctuated Tom's exclamation. "The young'uns will be happy about that. One to bottle-feed for sure. Our farm visitors will enjoy having a go at that too."

Finding the lamb's second leg folded between a sibling's forelegs, Harriet gently detangled it. Moments later, the lamb made its debut to the cheers of an audience, whose arrival Harriet hadn't been aware of until that moment. As Harriet wiped the little one's face, she spotted Doreen and Will. "How'd the puds come out?"

Doreen grinned. "As perfect as that lamb."

Will beamed at Harriet admiringly, and she felt heat creep into her face.

Pleased as punch, Harriet returned her attention to the next lamb. But the experienced mama didn't need any more help. Harriet remained at her side in case anything came up, but the rest of the delivery went smoothly.

Aunt Jinny donned her metaphorical physician's hat long enough to advise Doreen, "You might want to post signs outside the maternity barn advising expectant mums to mind where they go."

"Oh dear, yes. Thank you for the reminder. Your dad was always after me not to help with lambing or chores when I was pregnant."

Doreen's eldest daughter, thirteen-year-old Ava, snapped some photos of Harriet with the lambs. "These will be a hit on our social media. If that's okay with you, Dr. Bailey?"

"No problem."

"Be sure to tag Cobble Hill Veterinary Clinic," Will urged, shooting Harriet a wink.

Harriet's heart warmed at his thoughtfulness in ensuring that she might benefit from the advertising too. Thankfully, business had been steady over the past few weeks, and with lambing season almost upon them, she expected to be even busier. Although farmers were able to handle most complications, the sheer number of lambs due to be born in the area over the next three months meant there'd be more call for her specialized skills.

Harriet washed off as best she could with the bucket of warm soapy water Doreen's eldest son brought to her. "If it's okay with all of you, I'll zip home for a quick shower and change of clothes."

Despite living next door to the Danby farm, it was still more than half a mile from door to door, but thankfully she'd driven over. "I shouldn't be long."

"No problem. I'll keep everything warm until you return." Doreen herded her children toward the house, trailed by Will and Aunt Jinny.

Tom, who'd been trying to convince the ewe to take to all three of her lambs, finally conceded defeat and said he'd better fetch the wee one a bottle.

Harriet climbed into her ancient Land Rover. She still called it the Beast, although with a little more fondness than when she'd first arrived in White Church Bay. That had a lot to do with the fact that she'd grown adept at driving a stick shift, even on the steep hills about the Yorkshire countryside.

She'd scarcely driven a few hundred yards when a fox bolted across the road in front of her.

She stamped on the clutch and the brake simultaneously and threw the stick into neutral.

The animal made it across unscathed. But when it paused and her headlights caught the glint of its eyes, she wasn't sure it was a fox. She squinted through the side window for a better view. The last thing farmers needed worrying their sheep was a stray dog. Unfortunately, whatever it was disappeared through the hedgerow.

She drove the remaining distance to the cliffside property she'd inherited from her grandfather. The traditionally thatched carriage house at the front hosted the Bailey Art Gallery, which showcased her grandad's paintings for curious tourists, while Cobble Hill Veterinary Clinic occupied a portion of the main floor of the two-story house that sat behind the gallery, with Aunt Jinny's dower cottage next to it. A big barn sat off on the far side of the property, which she used for large animals in her care and occasionally for boarding clients' pets.

Harriet parked and climbed out of the Beast, frowning when Maxwell's barks greeted her from inside the house. The dachshund, whose hindquarters were paralyzed, managed to dash around the main floor thanks to the wheeled prosthesis her grandfather had gotten for him. He usually didn't make much of a fuss over her arrival, since he was used to her coming and going from the clinic throughout the day.

Hurrying inside, she gave him a reassuring pat. "Hey, what's the matter, boy?"

The dog calmed and led the way to the kitchen, clearly anticipating a treat. A moment later, Charlie, Cobble Hill's resident calico, sauntered in to make sure she didn't miss out. Purring loudly, she batted her bowl ahead of Maxwell's. What she lacked in traditional cuteness, thanks to scars sustained in a fire as a kitten, she made up for in personality. Harriet didn't mind. After all, Charlie had to live up to her name. Grandad had called all his office cats Charlie regardless of gender, saying that it gave him one less thing to remember.

Harriet humored the cat by adding the treats to her bowl first then gave Maxwell an extra one for chivalrously waiting his turn. Switching lights on as she went, Harriet dashed upstairs, grabbed a clean outfit, and hit the shower.

Right before she shut off the water, she heard Maxwell barking again. Grabbing a fluffy bath towel, she wrapped it around herself and opened the bathroom door. "Maxwell? What is it?"

The dog quieted, and a quick glance out the window confirmed no one had driven in. Harriet dried off and got dressed.

Again, she thought she heard Maxwell bark. *That sounds like an engine.* She hurried to a window that overlooked the parking area she shared with her aunt, but the Beast sat alone. Confused, she cocked her ear toward the hall. She could definitely hear an engine. It sounded as if it came from the rear of the property. Harriet high-tailed it to a window on that side of the house. The field that stretched from Aunt Jinny's cottage to the public cliffside path and North Sea beyond was shrouded in darkness.

Her pulse skipped. *Anyone could be out there, and I wouldn't know.* Kids sometimes raced dirt bikes along the cliff path, even though they weren't supposed to. And she didn't want to think about the unwelcome intruders they'd had around the house and out-buildings the past few months.

"Get a grip," she scolded herself, pivoting to peer out a side window. Faint lights from the Danbys' place winked comfortingly. Maybe the engine noise was from Tom starting a tractor.

Annoyed with herself for wasting so much time searching for the source of a phantom sound, Harriet returned to the ensuite bathroom—and tripped over something with a shriek. She grabbed the bedpost to keep from falling. "Charlie, you've got to stop sneaking up on me like that. Have you been bothering Maxwell too? Was that why he barked?"

Charlie darted under the bed and swatted at Harriet's foot as she walked by. But ten seconds later, barking erupted again. Harriet again dashed to the window overlooking the car park.

This time a streak of red light crossed the drapes as she pushed them aside. But when she peered down, she couldn't see any vehicles. She ran to the front of the house in time to see the dust from a large van driving away.

Thinking she might have missed hearing an emergency call, she checked her phone for messages. Nothing. "It couldn't have been too urgent," she muttered to Charlie, heading for the stairs. "Otherwise, with the Beast parked outside and the lights on in the house, they would have waited longer for me to get to the door. Just as well. Everyone will be waiting for me at the Danbys'."

Once downstairs, Harriet scratched behind Max's ears. "You tried to get my attention, didn't you, boy? Not to worry. Whoever it was is gone now." She grabbed her coat and keys and headed out.

She slowed as her truck lights swept across the side of the art gallery. The engine she'd heard had sounded as if it came from behind the building.

She drove a quick loop around the gallery to the barn. Nothing was there now. And it was too dark to see footprints or tire treads.

But what if her impromptu return had surprised yet another intruder? And what had they been doing there in the first place?

A NOTE FROM THE EDITORS

We hope you enjoyed another exciting volume in the Mysteries of Cobble Hill Farm series, published by Guideposts. For over seventy-five years, Guideposts, a nonprofit organization, has been driven by a vision of a world filled with hope. We aspire to be the voice of a trusted friend, a friend who makes you feel more hopeful and connected.

By making a purchase from Guideposts, you join our community in touching millions of lives, inspiring them to believe that all things are possible through faith, hope, and prayer. Your continued support allows us to provide uplifting resources to those in need. Whether through our communities, websites, apps, or publications, we inspire our audiences, bring them together, and comfort, uplift, entertain, and guide them. Visit us at guideposts.org to learn more.

We would love to hear from you. Write us at Guideposts, P.O. Box 5815, Harlan, Iowa 51593 or call us at (800) 932-2145. Did you love *On the Right Track*? Leave a review for this product on guideposts.org/shop. Your feedback helps others in our community find relevant products.

Loved Mysteries of Cobble Hill Farm? Check out some other Guideposts mystery series! Visit https://www.shopguideposts.org/fiction-books/mystery-fiction.html for more information.

SECRETS FROM GRANDMA'S ATTIC

Life is recorded not only in decades or years, but in events and memories that form the fabric of our being. Follow Tracy Doyle, Amy Allen, and Robin Davisson, the granddaughters of the recently deceased centenarian, Pearl Allen, as they explore the treasures found in the attic of Grandma Pearl's Victorian home, nestled near the banks of the Mississippi in Canton, Missouri. Not only do Pearl's descendants uncover a long-buried mystery at every attic exploration, they also discover their grandmother's legacy of deep, abiding faith, which has shaped and guided their family through the years. These uncovered Secrets from Grandma's Attic reveal stories of faith, redemption, and second chances that capture your heart long after you turn the last page.

History Lost and Found

The Art of Deception

Testament to a Patriot

Buttoned Up

Pearl of Great Price
Hidden Riches
Movers and Shakers
The Eye of the Cat
Refined by Fire
The Prince and the Popper
Something Shady
Duel Threat
A Royal Tea
The Heart of a Hero
Fractured Beauty
A Shadowy Past
In Its Time
Nothing Gold Can Stay
The Cameo Clue
Veiled Intentions
Turn Back the Dial
A Marathon of Kindness
A Thief in the Night
Coming Home